HEALTH HINTS FOR
FOUR-FOLD HEALTH

Teachings of
The Order of Christian Mystics

HEALTH HINTS FOR
FOUR-FOLD HEALTH

TEACHINGS OF THE ORDER OF CHRISTIAN MYSTICS

THE "CURTISS BOOKS" FREELY AVAILABLE AT

WWW.ORDEROFCHRISTIANMYSTICS.CO.ZA

HEALTH HINTS FOR
FOUR-FOLD HEALTH
FOR THE PURIFICATION AND HEALTH
OF THE BODY, MIND AND EMOTIONS

Transcribed by
HARRIETTE AUGUSTA CURTISS
and
F. HOMER CURTISS, B.S., M.D.
Founders of
THE ORDER OF CHRISTIAN MYSTICS
and
AUTHORS OF THE "CURTISS BOOKS"

2014 EDITION

REPUBLISHED FOR THE ORDER BY
MOUNT LINDEN PUBLISHING
JOHANNESBURG, SOUTH AFRICA
ISBN: 978-1-920483-12-8

"Ministers of Christ and Stewards of the Mysteries of God."

1 Corinthians 4 vs. 1

INTRODUCTION

We are constantly receiving letters from our students in all parts of the world asking for our prayers for their health. But as all of these letters show that the ill health is the result of wrong habits of life, diet and thought, we have assembled herein some simple general rules and practices which both scientific research and years of experience have proved essential to good health. Obviously, only the most essential facts and details can be given, hence we may disappoint those who place great emphasis on some one phase or fad, important though it may be for certain ends.

Body an Instrument.—First, it should be understood that since the body is the instrument through which the Soul contacts this earth plane, the Soul is limited in its expression by the kind of body in which it incarnates, and to its health, perfect development, training, and its responsiveness to the guidance of the indwelling Soul.

Health.—Second, it should be remembered that

perfect health is 100% functioning of all our organs
and tissues. Lack of health is merely a deficiency in
harmonious bodily functioning. The way to maintain
health is to stop making ourselves sick by wrong habits
of thought, emotion, diet and actions. Ill health is but a
symptom of broken law; the inability of the body to relieve its maladjustments and eliminate its poisons. Most
so-called treatment is but the palliation of symptoms
without the elimination of their fundamental causes.
Health means not merely freedom from disease but
freedom from fatigue, from the blues, and the negative and destructive emotions as well

Third, we reap the results of all we sow. If we violate
the laws of harmony in Nature, whether they be physical, mental, psychic or spiritual laws, we must expect
to reap corresponding inharmonious results.

Pain Necessary.—By unpleasant, even painful
symptoms, Nature gives us ample warning month after
month that something is wrong with our habits of life,
and that a change is necessary. Pain is often necessary for
self-preservation, through preventing excessive abuse
of the body leading to fatal conditions. If we do not heed
the warning, she does her best until so overcome that
she can no longer carry on. Then we pay attention, but
often only after great damage has been done and much

unnecessary suffering has been endured. Pain is valuable in calling man's attention to wrong conditions which should be remedied, not only by palliatives which merely mask the pain, but by change of habits.

Prayer.—While prayer and affirmations property invoked and sincerely *believed in* and *relied upon*, will always give at least temporary relief and help in time of trouble or suffering, and often miraculous cures because of great meritorious Karma, yet if the causes of that trouble or suffering are not stopped or eliminated, naturally they will continue to produce their unhappy results. Therefore, do not expect psychological or spiritual forces to give more than temporary relief, or to produce a permanent cure, unless you *change your habits of life* in such a way as to *eliminate the causes*, be they mental, emotional, psychic or physical. For instance, if you have a splinter in your finger, there is no use either denying that it is there, affirming that it will do no harm or praying to God to remove it for you. You have to recognize it for what it is and remove it yourself.

Immunity.—As we have said elsewhere: "You are normally immune to all diseases as long as your 'inner radiance,' your vitality or life-force is up to normal. But if it becomes depleted in any way — through overwork, exposure, wrong diet, inadequate elimination, worry, negative thoughts, destructive emotions, etc.,—then your normal rate of vibration is lowered, and the body then becomes a soil or 'culture medium' in which lower forms of life—germs, bacteria, nematodes, etc.,—can grow, and by their poisonous excretions—toxins—upset the whole system." [1]

The obvious thing to do, therefore, is to see that your vitality is always kept up to normal by removing all the factors that interfere with or lower it, whether they be structural, functional, toxic, dietetic, mental, emotional or psychic.

Disease.—Disease attacks only deficient tissues whose lowered vitality cannot resist the attack of other organisms, or fatigue, exposure or nerve exhaustion, etc. When not poisoned by the inadequate elimination of waste, and when properly nourished by rightly combined and properly masticated foods, and when controlled by constructive thoughts and emotions, you should never be tired, negative, sick, discouraged or subject to the blues. Normally you should be positive, cheerful, optimistic and happy, and capable of thinking clearly, making your decisions quickly, full of ambition and perseverance. All of these are the normal attributes of health.

Restoration.—All diseases, including angina, ane-

---

[1] See lesson *Fear Not*, Curtiss. Send for free copy.

mia, goitre, ulcers, tuberculosis, skin, kidney, liver, nervous diseases, etc., are but the end results of broken laws, whether of physical, chemical or mental unbalance, which permits them to manifest. They are all subject to restoration to normal through the *elimination of their causes* and the elimination of their effects. Since the cells die daily and hourly, we are reborn cell by cell daily, hence can build in new and disease-resisting cells until our entire body is made over in the image of the ideals we hold, and with the materials we furnish it through properly selected and properly combined foods.

Body Poisons.—The body usually expels violent poisons, but wrong food combinations produce mild poisons which accumulate and produce toxemia.

Four-Fold Health.—We wish to emphasize that perfect health must be four-fold, *i.e.*, physical, mental, emotional and spiritual. Treatment of any one phase alone is not sufficient for a permanent cure. Do not expect that treatment on any one plane will produce perfect results. The wrong habits of life on all four planes which are producing inharmony must be changed ere the causes will cease producing their unhappy effects.

CHAPTER I

MECHANICAL FACTORS IN HEALTH

Structural Defects.—Very few bodies are perfect in all their structural parts and functions. Many bodily ailments are due to organs or bones being out of place or sagging, often due to lack of tone because their nerve or blood supply is being interfered with. Usually this is due to slight displacements of the bones of the spine which press upon the nerves which come out from the spinal cord between them. For instance, sciatica is nearly always due to pressure on one of the nerve trunks forming the great sciatic nerve, after it branches off the spinal cord and passes between the bones of the spine. Also appendicitis is almost instantly relieved by the adjustment of the second lumbar vertebra, etc. Similar conditions of slight abnormal pressure occur frequently at the base of the brain, in the neck and anywhere else along the spine.

Adjustments.—Hence, a proper adjustment relieves the congestion and its symptoms almost immediately. The entire spine should be examined and adjusted by a chiropractor, osteopath, naturopath or other properly trained practitioner. Many of the younger and better trained practitioners protect you from wrong diagnosis by using the X-ray, neurocalometer and several other instruments to determine the exact condition before making the adjustments. As long as there is physical interference with the nerve and blood supply of the organs, nerves, endocrine glands, the brain or other structures, you cannot expect them to function normally. And if the glands do not function normally they produce deficient and abnormal products which are often irritating if not actually poisonous, and hence upset the entire body chemistry and functioning. Neither mind nor medicine can be curative if the cause is a mechanical one. The displacement must be corrected first.

Recurrence.—When not due to accidents, twists, strains, etc., most of these displacements are due to the irregular pull of muscular spasms, hence *tend to recur* until the cause of the irritated nerves is removed. Usually this is an acid or toxic condition which is relieved and only really cured, not by the adjustment, but by detoxication and proper diet.

Need for Exercise.—The body is a living organism which needs proper exercise of all its functions if they are to work together properly. Persons whose livelihood does not require much muscular exertion in the open air cannot properly oxidize much of their food without exercise, and without this all their functions tend to stagnate.

Object of Exercise.—The primary aim of exercise is not merely to strengthen the muscles used, but to stimulate the circulation, respiration and elimination. The increased activity quickens the heart beat, strengthens the heart muscle and flushes all the tissues with freshly aerated blood. The increased respiration draws more air into the lungs, thus enabling the blood to carry more oxygen to the tissues and produce heat and energy. It also purifies the blood by enabling it to throw off more gaseous waste products. The increased heat induces perspiration and thus increases elimination through the skin. Exercise also stimulates elimination through the bowels and kidneys, and tones up the whole body. Exercise also tends to correct slight dislocations of spine or other joints; and relaxes undue tension or contractual of muscles, thus giving equalization and poise. Persons who are weakened by illness, malignant diseases, tumors, ruptures and serious displacements should not exercise except under specialized directions. Do not take difficult or excessive exercise on a full stomach.

Outdoor Exercise.—One of the best of general exercises is to take a brisk walk of at least a mile or two in the open air each day. This may be taken to and from work, or at least part way. It should be brisk enough to produce a pleasing feeling of exertion and quickened pulse and respiration, but not far enough to produce fatigue. Swimming and games are also excellent exercises.

Rhythmic Walking.—Walking may be combined with mental and spiritual forces by the following exercise: As you stride along, rhythmically repeat some phrase which expresses your realization or need. For instance, inhale while you take four strides, mentally repeating, "I breathe in health," one word with each stride. During the next four strides exhale and repeat, "I breathe out waste," or "I am made pure." Repeat the phrase for some time during your walk. Next day take another phrase if desired, such as, "I breathe in love," during the inhalation, and "I breathe out blessing," on the exhalation.

Indoor Exercises.—The outdoor work may be supplemented by indoor exercises which involve bending, twisting and stretching at the waist, so that alternate pressure and stretching is brought upon the internal organs to squeeze out stagnant blood and suck in a fresh supply. This overcomes the congestion that occurs from lack of exercise, stimulates peristalsis, helps overcome constipation, etc. Such exercises can be found in any good book or magazine on health or physical exercise, although some sample exercises are given herewith. The best time for indoor exercise is on rising and just before retiring.

Sample exercises.—Repeat each of the following exercises seven times for the first week, then increase one more time each day until the amount desired is reached. Stop each time before becoming tired.

1. Swing the arms upward overhead, elbows straight. Bend forward and reach as far down to the toes as possible without bending the knees. Then swing arms back overhead. *Do not bend back backward,* but *stretch straight upward* and repeat.

2. With arms straight overhead, fingers locked, twist body to right, bend and try to touch the right ankle. Then stretch upward, twist to left and try to touch the left ankle.

3. With arms out shoulder high, twist body to right as far as possible. Twist back to front, stop and stretch. Then twist to left

4. With feet well spread and hands clasped over left shoulder, swing arms well down between the legs hard, as though chopping a block of wood. Swing the hands upward and outward diagonally to the right and up to the right shoulder. Repeat the downward swing and up on to left shoulder.

5. Lie flat on the back. Bend the knees up to the chest and give them a vigorous squeeze with the arms, and return to position.

6. Lie flat on the back. Reach right toe over left leg and touch the floor as far to the left as possible. Repeat seven times, then repeat to the right with the left toe. Keep shoulders flat on floor, twist only at the waist. Reduces hips.

7. Lie flat on the back. Keep the knees straight and lift them straight overhead. Take this gently at first. As your strength increases increase the number of times you take the exercise.

If any of these exercises, or the subsequent breathing exercises, make you dizzy, make your heart palpitate or give any unpleasant symptoms, stop at once and take fewer next time.

Bathing.—Whenever possible the exercises should be followed by a cool sponge or towel bath. A brisk shower or quick tub rinse may be preferred by those who are especially vigorous, but not for those beyond middle age. A towel partially wrung out of cool water will give all the needed stimulation. Begin by washing the face, neck and ears, then the arms, chest, back and legs in succession. Then take a coarse rough towel and rub the body briskly until the skin is dry and pink with the accelerated circulation. The value lies *not in the amount* of water used, but in its cool tonic effect and in the rubbing, in its effect on the pores, nerves and circulation. If this is done daily, a thorough soaking in a tub and scrubbing with soap will not be required more than once or twice a week.

Tonic Bath.—This bath cools down and soothes the nerves and parts involved, retards fermentation and gas formation, and stimulates elimination.

Draw three or four inches of cool water in the ordinary bath tub. *Sit down*, with the back leaning against a turkish towel hung over the slanting end of the tub. Keep the knees bent and spread so only the feet, seat and sexual organs will be in the water. Dash the water over the abdomen and rub it vigorously, also the sides and back as far as you can reach. Then lower the legs and dash the water over the upper part of the body. Step out of the tub and dry by rubbing vigorously with the bare hands only.[2]

Sun and Air Baths.—The value of frequent exposure of the skin to the air and sun is beyond the experimental stage in modern medicine. Aside from the increased metabolism and all the effects of chemical and physiological action of the actinic, infra-red and ultra-violet rays of the sun, exposure to light and air is stimulating to the mentally depressed, to the neurotic, the anemic and those suffering from melancholia, worry, lassitude and insomnia. It not only increases bodily tone and energy, but mental responses are brisker and mental activities are more

---

[2] *Orthodietetics*, Broughton, 145.

pronounced. Daily exposure of from five minutes at first may be gradually increased to several hours.

Nudism.—All the beneficial therapeutic effects, and also all that is essential in the physical and mental control of the passions, as advocated by the nudists, can be attained by familiarity with the sight of the exposed body while clad only in short trunks, such as men wear at most of the bathing beaches, but without the exposure of the sex organs themselves. Hence there is no *adequate excuse* for catering to exhibitionism through complete nudism.

CHAPTER II

BREATHING

Breathing.—There is a definite science of the breath into the technique of which we cannot enter in this short treatise. Such technical exercises should not be taken except under the personal guidance of a qualified teacher. Hence we will give only some simple fundamentals. The breathing exercise recommended while walking is given chiefly for its physical effect, that is, increasing the intake of oxygen and expelling as much of the volatile waste (gases) as possible. In sedentary work only about 10% of the air in the lungs is expelled in breathing, the rest being residual or dead air. Hence the necessity for deep breathing for complete aeration of the blood, as it takes at least ten full breaths to clear the lungs of the old stagnant, poison-laden air.

Uses of the Breath.—Never consciously use the breath without holding some constructive thought or idea; for what we hold in mind at that time is stamped upon the electrons of each cell. Happy, positive and constructive thoughts and emotions expand and illumine the electrons, while negative or destructive thoughts and emotions shrink and deaden them and retard or even pervert their proper functioning.

Changing the Rhythm.—To turn the normally unconscious function of breathing into a consciously directed function for definite ends, its rhythm must be altered. Breathing can be used to correlate mind and body, because it alters the circulation and brings more oxygenated blood to the brain. Slowing the rhythm of the breath slows the circulation to the brain and so calms both thoughts and emotions, and produces a quiet, calm mood, like pouring oil on troubled waters. Therefore, when mentally or emotionally excited, disturbed, worried or under a tension, sit down and relax all tension of body and take the following exercise.

Such frequent deliberate relaxation is a potent safeguard against fatigue and worry.

The Calming Breath.—Assume the posture for meditation as follows:

Sit in as quiet a place as possible where you can be free from interruption. Sit on a straight-backed chair, always in the same place and chair, facing the East, in the morning and the North in the evening. Allow the hands to rest comfortably on the thighs with the palms up and with the thumbs touching the tips of the first fingers.

Have the feet flat on the floor a few inches apart.

Sit with the head erect, the chin in and the spine straight. Do not let the back touch the chair. The position is exactly that in which the Egyptian statues are seated. The position should not be stiff or rigid, but comfortably erect and well poised and with the clothing loose.

Inhale slowly and quietly through both nostrils a comfortably deep, steady breath, with the mouth closed. First fill out the abdomen and then slowly fill up the lungs comfortably full, yet without tension or straining.

Be careful that the muscles of the neck and throat are not tense or rigid. To be sure of this, turn and bend the head from side to side for a moment to remove all strain and rigidity.

Pulse Rate.—Use your normal pulse-rate to give your rhythm. Inhale quietly for 6, 8 or 10 heartbeats. Hold the breath for half the number of intake counts—3, 4 or 5—then completely empty the lungs during the same number of counts as used during the intake. Hold the breath out and the lungs empty for half the exhalation counts, then slowly and rhythmically begin to inhale again. After you have learned your rhythm, you will not need to distract your attention from the object of the breath by counting. When you exhale, relax completely, and let go all tension of body and mind.

What to Think.—As we have said elsewhere:

"During the inhalation hold the thought that you are breathing in the forces of love, strength, courage and purity or any other virtue you desire; that during the pause they are filling you full to overflowing,"[1] and that during the outbreathing you are breathing out all your troubles, anxieties and cares, and dissipating them like exhaust steam. Repeat this from seven to fifteen times or until you feel relaxed and calm. At any time of day or night when you find yourself hurried, worried or under a nervous strain, sit down quietly and practice this relaxation and quietness. The power of this simple exercise to calm and restore the normal rhythm to both body and mind will scarcely be believed by those who have not tried it. It alone can calm an agitated mind or cheer a sad heart and restore one to peace and harmony with the world.

The Cleansing Breathe.—Inhale slowly your regular number of counts. Hold the breath for half that number of counts and then exhale it in seven *short expulsive puffs*, with the lips puckered as if about to whistle. As you exhale, relax your erect position, allowing the lungs to deflate and collapse, while the body slumps forward in complete relaxation as the last bit of breath is exhaled. Thea raise the body to its erect posture again and repeat.

Think.—During the inhalation, hold the thought

---

[1] *The Voice of Isis*, Curtiss, 351.

that you are drawing in Divine Love, Infinite Life, Perfection and Spiritual Power which shall fill your aura to overflowing and wash out, and also protect you, from all inharmony or danger, and also conquer all obstacles. This breath starts all the vital energies into activity all over the body to purify it by dissolving and washing out all poisonous waste materials. Therefore, hold the thought of its purifying and uplifting you in body as well as in mind.

With each outward puff hold the thought that you are expelling all mental irritations, inharmonies, impurities and imperfections that you have recognized during your period of self-examination the night before, together with anything disagreeable that you may have dreamed about or experienced during the night.

Since this exercise increases the elimination of waste materials, quite naturally one of its first effects will be to stir up the wastes in your body which have been allowed to accumulate more or less. Hence you should be especially careful to use proper food combinations, plenty of green vegetables, especially natural laxatives,[2] etc., also a glass of water or fruit juice every three hours or so between meals during the day in order to stimulate and facilitate elimination. Repeat this *Cleansing Breath* seven times or until you feel cleansed and purified. If you feel dizzy, stop and rest awhile.

---

[2] See page 26-7.

Prana.—But there are other life-forces in the air besides the oxygen. There is the vital life-force of the ethers which is called *prana*. This force can be consciously drawn in, absorbed and used to charge the body with life-force or vitality so that it will prevent fatigue, resist disease, endure extremes of heat and cold and change the tone of your thoughts and emotions, and hence of your bodily reactions.

Vitalizing Breath.—Whenever tired, debilitated, discouraged, weak or negative, you can charge your body with the vital, energizing life-force of prana by taking the following exercise. Make a habit of doing this *every morning* after your bath, breathing and prayers, whether you feel that you need it especially or not.

Stand facing the East, in the sunlight if possible. Hold the arms forward shoulder high, with the palms facing outward toward the Sun. Hold the head level, but turn the eyes upward as though you were looking through your eyebrows. This brings the proper tension on the optic nerve. As you slowly inhale your normal number of counts, draw the hands straight back until they are opposite the sides of the shoulders, but with the palms still facing forward. Have the shoulder blades touching in the back.

Think.—As you inhale, hold the thought that you are drawing in the currents of Divine life (prana) through the center between the eyebrows (Adjna) toward which you are looking. See it pouring in as a stream of radiant white light which fills your body full to overflowing. Hold the breath half the number of inhalation counts, and as you exhale and relax, gently flood the entire body with its life-giving radiance and warmth. Repeat seven times the first week, then increase one time each day until twenty-one is reached. This will so charge your body with dynamic life-force and magnetism that you will be able to meet all the conditions and problems of the day with a positive attitude and under the guidance of the Christ within. Realize that your elimination, and the inflow of the spiritual forces, makes die body more resistant to all forms of inharmony, weariness, sickness and disease. For no disease can attack a body that is normal in tone and radiating positive vitality. Try it and prove it, then use it daily.

Transmuting Breath.—If troubled with excessive congestion of the sex centers, or thoughts thereof, remember that all glands are stimulated *by thought* as well as contact, just as your mouth waters at the thought of food. To maintain control, deliberately *turn your thoughts* to other things or perform *some kind of creative work* with hands or mind. Also you may sit facing the East and use the following *Prayer to the Divine Mother*.

Prayer.—O Divine Mother! Illumine me with Divine Wisdom, vivify me with Divine Life and purify me with Divine Love, that in all I think and say and do I may be more and more Thy child.[3]

Then as you inhale rhythmically draw the forces from the base of the spine and surrounding region up through the central canal of the spinal cord to the center of the brain (Sahasrara). Hold them there during the pause, and exhale them through the center in the forehead (Adjna). Repeating this from seven to twenty-one times, or more if necessary, will lift up the forces and give quick relief and a sense of lightness, purity and power.

Spiritualizing Breath.—When in special need of spiritual power, use the following

Prayer for Realization.—O Eternal Being! Thou ever Living One! Thou loving I Am Presence, whose I Am and whom I serve! Thou art anchored in me and I in Thee. Thou art mine and I am Thine. Thou art my eternal pattern. Make me more and more like Thee.

Then breathe rhythmically. As you inhale draw down a ray of brilliant white light from your radiant I Am Presence, or Higher Self, through the top of the head (Sahasrara). Hold it in the center of

---

[3] For further details see *The Message of Aquaria*, Curtiss, 433.

your brain during the pause, and as you exhale focus it in your heart until it becomes a glowing ball of dazzling white light whose radiance fills your whole body. Repeat seven to twenty-one times or until thoroughly charged with the warm glow of the spiritual fire.

CHAPTER III

CONSTIPATION

Auto-toxemia.—One vitally important and almost universal factor in ill health is constipation. This permits continuous absorption of poisons from the intestines and produces auto-toxemia which is the greatest underlying cause of all diseases.

Peristalsis.—As the undigested remnants of the food, such as all cellulose or the structural fibers of vegetables, called roughage, pass along the intestines, all the digestible elements and fluids are continually being absorbed. But if the bowel movement—called peristalsis—is sluggish, the bacteria normally present to help disintegrate the food are reinforced by putrifying bacteria, and the sluggish movement of the debris, gives the latter time to multiply and produce their poisonous toxines and gases—indol, skatol, etc.

Putrifaction.—Unless these gaseous products and toxines are promptly eliminated, they are absorbed by the blood and thus poison the entire system, often in such quantity that they are exhaled as bad odors—so-called halitosis—through the breath, but only after they have bathed and poisoned all the tissues of your body, including the brain.

Therefore, when you are constipated *every cell* and tissue and organ is also constipated and clogged up with uneliminated or reabsorbed poisons. These may produce mental sluggishness or brain fag, even temporary insanity; nearly all insane persons are badly constipated. Headaches, neuralgia and rheumatic pains that are considered only local are merely symptoms of the filth that has been absorbed from the colon. Therefore, regular, full and free bowel movements, at least two or three times a day, are essential and *basically important*. Do not expect perfect health without them.

Lactic Add.—Lactic acid destroys the putrifying bacteria and promotes the growth of the helpful, symbiotic bacteria. Hence the frequent use of sour milk, clabber or buttermilk, which contain lactic acid forming bacteria—bacillus acidophilus and b. bifidus—help to purify the bowels and reduce putrifaction, hence tend to longevity.

Bulk.—There should be sufficient bulk of undigestible residue to slightly distend the bowels and give them something for the muscles to work on and push along. Bulk is also needed to gather up and sweep out particles of residue too small to be pushed along by themselves. This bulk is usually supplied by the undigestible cellulose, lignin, xylose, etc., particularly of the leafy greens such as spinach, kale, beet and turnip tops, dandelion, etc., as well as celery, cabbage, broccoli, sauerkraut, parsnips, squash, etc. Where this bulk is insufficient it can be supplied by the use of substitutes of little or no food value, but which swell and give great bulk, such as the sea-weed, agar, Irish moss, flax or psyllium seed or preparations thereof such as Konsyl, Kondremul, etc. But these adjuvants should be taken either with, or *immediately after* the meal so they will *mix with remnants of the food* and help pass it along, otherwise they may form lumps by themselves and thus cause obstruction.

Fluids.—Another important factor is sufficient fluids. All foods must be digested into a fluid state before they can be absorbed into the blood which carries them to the tissues. This requires considerable water or other fluids. While the digestive juices should not be unduly diluted during meals, at least one cup of soup or other fluid should be taken with or after each-meal. But each mouthful of food should be thoroughly chewed to a thin cream and not be washed down with drink. Since the fluids are rapidly absorbed during the first two hours after a meal, there is usually left in the stomach a residue which is too thick to be absorbed without dilution. Therefore, always take a glass of water an hour and a half to two hours after each meal.

B. O.—Since the body is two-thirds water by weight, and is constantly losing it by excretion and evaporation, unless it is frequently replenished the perspiration becomes odorous—commonly called "B.O.," or body odor—the urine becomes scanty, concentrated and often irritating. If water is not furnished freely, it will be absorbed from the colon, along with its acids and toxins, leaving the bowels dry and constipated. Therefore, make a regular practice of drinking a glass of water or fruit or vegetable juice every three hours. Always stop in mid-morning and mid-afternoon for your drink.

Thinned Blood.—The water is absorbed directly into the blood, so that within a half hour after drinking you have a half pint more blood. It is therefore that much thinner and more fluid, and hence is more able to wash out the waste products from the tissues and eliminate them. As you sip the water, hold the mental picture of its flowing right through you, washing out both your tissues and your bowels.

The excessive drinking—16 to 24 glasses—advocated by some, only stimulates rapid excretion and puts an unnecessary strain on the kidneys, but at least six to eight glasses of fluids-should be taken daily.

Laxative Food.—In addition to the beneficial results of both bulk and fluids, certain foods chemically stimulate the peristaltic action of the bowels and so push the debris along more rapidly. Among such foods are most fresh fruits, particularly figs, prunes,[1] grapes, cherries, etc. Among the vegetables, all the leafy or salad vegetables, and onions, are also laxative. On the other hand, cheese and berries, particularly blackberries, are constipating. In fact, an old-time remedy for diarrhoea is blackberries or a tea made from their dried leaves. But *diarrhoea should not be checked* until after a large dose of Pluto Water or salts has been taken to sweep out the irritating cause.

Habit.—Another helpful factor is habit. Always go to the stool as soon as the impulse comes. If put off over a few minutes the impulse may pass by and disappear for hours, thus allowing accumulation and absorption to take place. *Never neglect a call of Nature.* Excuse yourself and go at once. Let other things wait. This is vitally important if you ever expect to be cured.

Train the Subconscious.—Unless you have two or more regular, soft and *effortless* evacuations each day, you are constipated.

Therefore, train the subconscious mind to be ready to evacuate regularly at certain times of day. *Go regularly* at those times and do the best you can without undue straining, until the habit is estab-

---

[1] Use Santa Clara prunes if possible, as they are said to be less acid-forming.

lished of having a perfect stool at that hour. Undue straining is apt to bring on piles or hemorrhoids when the colon is congested. A perfect stool should be so soft that it is barely formed, about the shape of a good sized banana, and should leave the rectum as clean and free as your esophagus is after swallowing.

Simple Enema.—A simple enema is a pint or two of water which simply washes out lower bowel or rectum. Even if you have a perfect stool every day, there are many pockets in the intestines where feces may collect in large masses. Therefore, make a regular practice of washing out, not merely the rectum but the entire colon. This will wash out the acids and toxines, even if there is but little solid matter to remove. Repeat this daily until you have two movements a day besides the enema.

Accumulations.—If accumulations occur, even though a small amount is discharged from the lower end of the colon daily, the bowel still remains clogged by more waste flowing into it at the upper end. Hence constipation may be persistent and continuous in spite of some daily discharge. Long retention of this filth allows it to harden, forming dry incrustations which often adhere to the bowel walls sometimes for months and years, stretching the colon to two or three times, its normal size. Cases have been known to measure 18 inches in circumference, resembling a tumor, and containing as much as two gallons of festering filth. The high enema should be continued until no more solids come away.

Purgatives.—A colon that is constantly whipped into action by some irritating drug sooner or later becomes torpid and insensitive to the expulsion stimulus of its normal contents and so acquires a functional paralysis. The more irritating or "active" the drug, the more profound the exhaustion of the sensitivity ultimately becomes.

Spastic Colon.—On the other hand, the continued use of purgatives may be so irritating as to cause "spastic colon," in which condition the bowel is in a state of more or less constant contraction. This lessens the size and motility of the bowel and adds to the constipation.

High Colonic.—Since in all diseased conditions there is both acidosis and auto-toxemia, and especially when masses have accumulated, a special type of enema, called a "high colonic," is required. This is needed, not merely to flush out the lower rectum, but must contain enough water to fill the entire colon—descending, transverse, ascending—way over to the appendix on the lower right side of the abdomen. This large amount of water is needed gradually to dissolve the accumulated masses from which so much toxic absorption has been continually taking place, and wash them out. For when the bowel has been greatly stretched by accumulations it cannot empty itself.

Prevent Absorption.—To prevent absorption from the toxins dissolved by the high colonic, at least two to four glasses of water, preferably hot for its relaxing effect, should be drunk *before* taking the colonic. Otherwise, reactions such as headache, dizziness, etc., may follow the enema.

Method.—While the lower rectum may be washed out while in a sitting posture, the posture used for the high colonic is of great importance. The water should always flow downward or it cannot get by the kinks caused by the accumulations or the sagging organs. First wash out the rectum and then take a

Knee-chest Position.—Get down on your knees on a rug, keeping the hips high and touching the rug with your left shoulder and side of face, and leaving your right hand free to manipulate the tube. If too weak for this, lie on the left side or on the back with the hips considerably elevated.

Preparation.—Then prepare 2 to 3 quarts of water as hot (105° to 106°) as the hand can remain in comfortably, to which a teaspoonful of soda has been added. The water rapidly puts the poisons in solution and unless the soda is used they may be absorbed sufficiently to cause headache, dizziness or other unpleasant symptoms. The *drinking beforehand* and the soda prevent this.

Injection.—Empty the rectum by injecting about a pint and letting it out. Then inject slowly as much as you can hold comfortably *without a spasm of ejection*, then massage the bowels upward on the left side, then let in more water and massage across the stomach and down on the right side until you can feel the water reach down to the appendix. If a spasm of expulsion occurs, as soon as you feel it coming on, shut off the water and hold it in tight until the spasm passes away without ejecting any water. Then turn on the water again until you have taken as much as can be absorbed without pain.

Expulsion.—The expulsion will come in mild spasms or waves, but it may take fifteen or twenty minutes for the water that was way over to the appendix to come down, so have patience and wait without straining.[1] When you are sure the last has come away, then inject another quart of cool water (65° to 70°) to tone up the muscles of the bowel so they will learn to work normally without depending upon the enema or colonic for natural evacuation.

Frequency.—Take this high colonic every night for a week or ten days until your toxic symptoms disappear and you are sure all the old accumulations have been softened up and eliminated. After that do not miss one at least once or twice a week for the rest of your life. You will notice a distinct improve-

---

[1] Walking about will help bring on the expulsion.

ment in your mental and emotional reactions, as well as in your physical condition, as soon as you begin.

The Purge.—Since all acute and chronic disorders have as their background and basic cause—when not mechanical or due to deformity—a long continued accumulation of acids and toxins, the cells of all the tissues of the body are loaded with those negative and debilitating substances. "The object of the purge is not merely to move the bowels and get rid of the solid wastes, but to wash from the body its acid-laden fluids: serum from the blood, lymph from the tissues, and accumulated toxines from the intestines. The thirst resulting from this dehydration will make the free use of fruit juices very gratifying.[2] Thus an alkaline or baseforming source of supply is formed to replenish its deficient stores; and the condition of the body immediately is one of lowered acidity, or rather a heightened alkalinity—hence the feeling of relief that usually follows this rather drastic purging."[3]

Dose.—On arising take three Seidlitz powders 20 minutes apart the first day, two the second day and one the third day. *Fast from everything but fruit juices*—unsweetened orange, lemon or grapefruit, or alternated with grape or pineapple juice if desired—during the purge. Take an enema nightly.

---

[2] While undergoing a purge or when fasting, do not swallow any saliva, as it carries off many poisons.
[3] *A New Health Era*, Hay, 142-3.

Crisis.—This stirs up so much of the stored-up acid and toxines that reactionary symptoms called a "crisis" may be experienced while they are being eliminated in such great quantities. This may include headache, dizziness, nausea, even skin eruptions and symptoms of the major diseases you have had even years ago a trace of which has been left in your system. So be faithful in keeping up the three day purge until completed.

Return to Diet.—The return to normal diet should be gradual. Keep on with nothing but fruit juices *until hunger returns*, as it will when the detoxication is sufficiently complete, even if you eat no solid food for a week or two.

The Hay plan is as follows: The first *two days* afterward eat only broth,[1] salad with dressing and a fruit for dessert. For the next *three days* use broth, salad, one cooked vegetable, and a fruit dessert. For the main meal for the *next week*, broth, salad, two cooked vegetables, fruit dessert. The next two weeks, broth, two cooked vegetables, bacon if desired, fruit dessert. Then you may have the first starch meal of broth, vegetable salad, two cooked vegetables, whole baked potato and a sweet dessert (No acid in dressing or dessert, as this is a starch meal.) After this you can return to full diet as below of broth or soup, salad (fruit or vegetables), two cooked vegetables, meat, fish, eggs, or any other

---

[1] The word broth always refers to vegetable broth.

protein, fruit or acid dessert. After the first two days you may have milk (sweet, buttermilk or clabber) with your fruit juice for breakfast.

Full Diet.—After returning to full diet, plan four protein and three starch meals per week, selecting foods that will give you 80% alkaline forming food and 20% or less acid-forming, the proportion required to keep your body in health.[3]

As the skin is also eliminating freely during the purge, at least a sponge bath should be taken daily or oftener. A one day purge and fast should be taken at least once a month.

Habit Forming.—"Patients are sometimes cautioned by medical doctors to avoid enemas lest a habit be formed. But if it is a habit, it is a cleanly one and conducive to health and normality. People have used the enema daily for more than fifty years, and it has kept them young, active and free from disease."[4] Constipation, also an over-full bladder, stimulate excessive sex desires by their congestion of the surrounding pelvic region.

Outgrowing Its Use.—With proper food combinations, fluids and exercise, when once regulated, there will be no constipation, hence no need for the enema, only the weekly high colonic.

Examination.—If the measures recommended herein do not relieve the condition, examination

---

[3] See page 109.
[4] *How to Live Magazine*, April 1936, 18.

should be made for strictures, adhesions, kinks, chronic contractions, foreign bodies or tumors which may be mechanically obstructing the bowels.

Mosquito Bites.—Mosquito, flea bites and even bee and nettle stings, also poison ivy, cause little swelling, itching or inconvenience if you are not acid or toxic.

Odors.—To neutralize odors in the bathroom or elsewhere, roll up a sheet of toilet or other paper into a tight taper and light it. As it burns wave it slowly through the air in all parts of the room and the odors will be neutralized. Drop the end of the taper into the toilet before it burns your fingers.

The Use of Salts.—Since acidosis and toxemia are present to some extent in all diseased conditions, their elimination is the first step toward cure. Therefore, in practically all cases—except appendicitis, stomach or intestinal ulcers, cancer, etc.—the saline purge is of primary importance and should be the first thing to start. *Follow the directions* given on pages 32 and 33 *exactly* and *persistently*.

Gas-formation.—Do not be discouraged if gas-formation continues for some time while the digestive system is being re-educated. If it persists, try chopping the vegetables very fine or making a puree of them, so as to decrease the irritation of too coarse particles.

CHAPTER IV

ACUTE DISEASES

Colds.—Dr. Hay tells us that: "Colds are not *caught*. They are accumulated with the feet under the table, and in no other way."[1] Colds, sinusitis, tonsillitis, fevers and diseases of the respiratory tract follow overeating and toxic absorption from the bowels. Toxines impair the nourishment of all tissues, devitalizing especially the mucous membranes through which they are excreted, and thus allowing bacteria to invade the tissues and the system.

Acute Diseases.—At the *first sign* of lassitude, headache, sore throat, cold, running nose, cough, fever, stomach or bowel trouble, *stop eating* and begin a purge. The old adage, "*If* you feed a cold, you'll have a fever to starve," is a well known fact. The main idea is to *stop food* and *eliminate* in every way, through bowels, kidneys and skin. Immediately take a generous dose of the purge, then take a high enema *every three hours* while awake the first day, even if, and *especially if*, the patient is in

---

[1] *The New Health Era*, Hay, 148.

a coma. Repeat the enema night and morning each day afterward *in addition* to the purge.

Citrus Flush.—Add a rounded teaspoonful of soda to the juice of a whole lemon. After the foaming has subsided, add the mixture to two glasses of hot water. Immediately sip it as rapidly as you can drink it comfortably until the entire amount is consumed and a good sweat is started. Hold the idea that the liquid is going right into the blood stream, thus thinning it and making it more capable of dissolving and flushing out the impurities through the skin, kidneys and bowels, while the lemon juice will help to neutralize the acids and toxines. Then drink a glass of water, or fruit juice if desired, every hour while awake to keep up the flushing process.

Hot Pack.—If the attack starts with a toxic chill, that is not relieved by a hot enema, immediately after the enema take a hot bath containing four cupfuls of Epsom Salts. Or instead, take a hot wet pack, as follows: Fold a sheet to the width that will reach from the armpits to the hips. Wring it out in water as hot as the hands can be held in, and wrap it around the body. Wrap around this a dry sheet folded wide enough to overlap the wet sheet. Wrap up in a blanket and allow it to remain on from two to eight hours or until sweating has ceased. Then remove and sponge with tepid water. Let the patient have no food, only water or fruit juices, until returning *hunger calls* for food, even if the fast lasts *a week or two*. Begin feeding as directed after the purge on page 33.

Infantile Paralysis.—Attacks of flu or of infantile paralysis treated in this way and without medication will seldom have any or at least only temporary paralysis.

Appendicitis.—Attacks of appendicitis should NOT be given a purge or *anything at all* by mouth, not even water. Put an ice bag over the appendix and take a high enema *every two hours*. Usually unloading the bowel relieves the pain and causes the temperature to drop within a half hour, and the acute attack is over within two hours. Most patients are up and often at work the next day. Dr. Hay has treated over five hundred cases this way *without a single death*, while the death rate from operation is seldom less than 30% to 40%.

Ruptured.—Even when the appendix is ruptured, the inflammatory adhesions thrown out by the bowel will wall in the pus and keep it from causing a general peritonitis until the mass ruptures *into the bowel* and is washed out by the daily enema. Of course, this is heresy from a surgical standpoint, but the proof of its soundness is the results. What surgeon can match Dr. Hay's record of over five hundred cases and *thirty ruptured* appendices *without a single death*? Acute attacks of other diseases yield corresponding results; if the above mentioned procedure is faithfully followed, recovery taking place even before the trouble is sufficiently established to be diagnosed.

Operations.—"To lose the tonsils or appendix is to place the body under a permanent handicap, that will interfere with function in some or many ways so long as you live.

"Constipation follows the removal of the appendix as effect follows cause; also the absence of tonsils opens the way for all sorts of infection later on."[2]

Abscesses.—"Internal abscesses, inflammations, infiltrations, adhesions, have disappeared with monotonous regularity when the whole man was subjected to radical detoxication and dietary correction. No case of duodenal ulcer has failed to entirely recover.

"Pneumonia, erysipelas, typhoid fever, influenza, acute arthritis, colitis, hay fever, all subside when the body is fairly detoxicated and the diet so corrected as to stop this excessive formation of the acid end-products."[3]

[2] *The New Health Era*, Hay, 197. See also page 54.
[3] *The New Health Era*, Hay, 198, 144, 142.

CHAPTER V

FOOD IN GENERAL

Intemperance.—Intemperance in eating probably causes more unnecessary suffering than intemperance in drink. Excessive food overwhelms the system with imperfectly oxidized and toxic products.

Faulty diet and improper elimination are probably the most prolific physiological causes of lack of health, hence we will go into some detail concerning them.

Food.—While individual idiosyncracies vary widely—even bringing over pet tastes or instinctive aversions and habits from past lives—nevertheless there are certain mechanical and chemical laws which must be observed if the complex mixture of the chemical products which result from digestion are to be blended compatibly with each other and not produce abnormal products whose harmful results are grouped under the general term of acidosis.

Recent researches and laboratory tests have proved the possibility of indefinitely prolonging life through complying with the laws of life. Therefore, there is no reason for early death (barring accident) except through ignorance of and failure to conform to the laws of hygiene, scientific dietetics and right thinking.

Human Classes.—Hindu philosophy classifies human beings into three types, the ignorant (*Tamasik*), the passionate (*Rajasic*) and the spiritual (*Sattvic*). The ignorant, who function largely on the plane of gross animal existence, are stupid and have little power of discrimination between that which is desirable and undesirable. Such tend to indiscriminate eating without regard to cleanliness or purity—stale, partly putrid, and unclean foods—and gluttony, and are subject to all manner of morbid appetites, thoughts and destructive emotions. The passionate type craves animal foods, and foods that are pungent, bitter, saline, sour, overhot, icecold, spicy, etc. The spiritual (Sattvic) type possess an innate discrimination in everything pertaining to their lives, not only thoughts and emotions, but also foods, naturally tending to choose that which is pure and healthful and conducive to peace, harmony and health. But even this class often errs through ignorance of the fundamental chemical laws which are presented herewith.[1]

Spiritual Seekers.—Those who are consciously seeking their spiritual unfoldment should choose largely the Sattvic foods, or combinations of well

---

[1] *Hindu Dietetics*, "Sri Sukul", 1.

chosen Rajasic foods, avoiding the Tamasic as much as possible. While spiritual unfoldment does not come from the stomach, but from the heart, nevertheless, what and how you eat does affect your mental and emotional states, hence should be wisely planned. Thus the craving for particular kinds of food depends upon the stage of evolution of the individual. But if you have a craving for a special food, it is well to satisfy that craving, but subject to moderation and the laws of chemical compatibility.

Chemical Classes.—Chemically, foods are classified as acid-forming, base-forming[2] or neutral. Most acid fruits and green vegetables are base-forming after they are digested, hence neutralize the effects of the acid-forming foods, *i.e.*, starches, cereals, flour products, etc.—and proteins—meat (except bacon), fish, egg whites, cheese (except cream cheese), milk, nuts (except almonds).

Since the body is normally 80% alkaline and only 20% acid, your diet should be so selected as to be composed of 80% alkaline, or base-forming foods, and only 20% starch and proteins, both of which form acid after digesting.[3] On the basis of calories, only 10 calories out of every 100 should be proteins.

Proteins.—Dr. William Howard Hay estimates that we eat ten times as many proteins as we need.

---

[2] Alkaline-forming.
[3] See chart on page 109.

This excess not only puts extra work on die kidneys and liver, but over stimulates the circulation and produces an organic strain so that the "factor of safety" of these organs may be exceeded and their collapse result.

Proteins also produce the most irritating debris which both clog the system and irritate the mucous membrane of the organs of elimination. Another source of great acid formation is the use of refined and bleached white flour products and white sugar. Great acidity comes both from too much of the wrong type of food and from *wrong combinations*.

Catarrh.—Catarrhal conditions of nose, throat, sinuses, stomach, intestines, etc., pass through three stages, (a) congestion or inflammation, (b) mucous or dripping excretion, and (c) dry or crust stages. But all will disappear when their mucous membranes are relieved of the irritation of acid end-products of digestion and auto-toxemia through thorough detoxication, fasting and proper diet. Germs of colds and other infections are always present in the mouth and nasal passages, but they cannot grow if the vitality of the tissues is not depleted by acidosis and toxemia or by destructive mental and emotional storms.

Old Age.—"The life processes produce poisons as by-products, of their activity. We almost always do die of poisons! The only real exception is when we are killed by physical violence—poison, therefore, is the main factor in causing old age and death. How extremely important it is to reduce our daily dose of poison and eliminate as thoroughly and promptly as possible all such poisons."[3]

Passions Stimulated.—That a high-protein or meat diet tends to intensify lower animalistic impulses and passions, while a low-protein, vegetarian diet tends to reduce them, has been known since the most ancient times. The Greek Orphists, the Pythagoreans, the Manichaeans, the Neo-Platonists, the Trappist monks and nearly all religious orders practicing monasticism abstained from foods rich in proteins—among the Pythagoreans including beans!—with that end in view. Modern records show that the use of protein-rich, uric-acid-forming foods which acidify the blood and urine, increase the blood pressure, and therefore heighten sexual desire through their irritating effect upon the mucous membranes of the genital organs. Spices, pepper, tobacco, pickles, shellfish and alcohol have a similar sexually stimulating effect due to their irritation of the mucous membranes.

Low   Protein   Diet.—Experiments   of   the Carnegie Institute of Washington[4] in 1919 with two squads of twelve men each over a period of four

---

[3] *How to Live*, Fisher, 61.
[4] *Human Vitality md Efficiency under Prolonged Restricted Diet*. Publication, 280.

months showed a lowered blood pressure in those on a low-protein diet, while the reduction in or extinction of their sex desire and its usual manifestations in dreams and habits and their mental attitude toward women was of a striking nature. Even the sex-appeal of dancing with women was either entirely absent or negligible. After the second or third day after the return to uncontrolled rich-protein diet, the former sex impulses and experiences returned, thus showing the specific influence of rich-protein diet on sex.

Periodic Functions.—Such diet has a similar influence on the periodic functions of women, a low-protein and simple, non-stimulating diet greatly relieving if not removing most of the symptoms. This women can easily prove for themselves.

Puberty.—The same rule applies to certain bad habits in young people. During the rapid development of the sexual system throughout puberty, chemical stimulation of the organs can be avoided and the desire for gratification largely eradicated by a low-protein diet. "Especially avoid overeating, and all foods tending towards acidity, toxemia and especially towards constipation. So many parents teach their children the principles of chastity, and virtue in the nursery and yet unwittingly stimulate their passions at the table."[5]

---

[5] For further details see *Diet and Sex*, Siegmeister, 50¢.

Diversion.—Both constipation and an over-full bladder cause pressure and congestion of the pelvic region, and hence stimulation of the sex centers. Plenty of outdoor exercise, but especially active interest in using the creative force in *making things* with the hands or mind, will divert the attention and the force from these centers.

Endurance.—The endurance tests conducted by Prof. Irving Fisher with Yale athletes at the Battle Creek Sanitarium years ago were all won by a wide margin by the vegetarians. This shows that a high-protein diet also decreases endurance and produces toxines, and helps bring about deposits, while a low-protein diet increases endurance and keeps the system free from toxines and mineral deposits.

Undesirable Foods.—Among the worst foods are anything with an offensive or spoiled odor, such as certain old or "sharp" cheeses, "high" poultry, game or odorous fish or shell-fish, also sweetbreads, liver, kidneys and brains. Excessive use of fish especially raw, as in the Hawaiian Islands—tends to the development of skin diseases, such as ulcers, rashes, leprosy, etc. This also applies to nations which eat a great deal of salted, pickled or smoked fish, such as the Scandinavians.

Appetite.—The needs of individuals vary. Eat the kind and quantity of food your appetite craves, after a thorough purging has restored your true hunger, but *combine it correctly*. Do not "fill up" the stomach just from force of habit, and always stop eating *while* you are enjoying the food, and respect the variation in amount as the animals do, according to appetite, a little at one meal, none at another. Especially avoid any food for which you have an aversion, for your subconscious or animal-soul knows what is best for you.

Feeding Children.—Do not compel children to eat, especially things which they dislike. Life-long aversions may thus be formed. Let their hunger guide. Do not try to "clean up your plate," nor force children to do so. Undesired food is far better left out of your stomach than in.—You are not "saving it" by eating it, only putting extra work on the organs of elimination. Eliminate it by not eating it. To restore lost appetite, drop out a meal or two. Animals refuse all food when ill. *So should you.*

Fasting.—*Do not hesitate to fast* from all solid food until your hunger *demands* food, but drink plenty of water or, better still, fruit juices meanwhile, even if the fast last for *days and weeks*. Far better eat too little than too much. A purge and a fast of a week or two will cure most functional diseases.

"Epileptics have fasted for a month and never again suffered a return of the convulsions. Nephritis, diabetes, skin diseases, asthma, all recover in the absence of all food; also all other diseases resulting from wrong chemistry will readjust themselves when the body is free to give all its attention to cleaning house."[6]

Life-force.—Remember that food is not the source of your life-force. That comes from God through your astral body. Food, water and air are but materials and energy-fuels needed to replace those used up by the expression of your life and consciousness through the body. Proteins and minerals replace the tissues used up. As these die and need replacement at an even rate, whether we are active or sedentary, according to Dr. Hay we all need proteins according to our *size*, not according to our activity. Since starch, sugars and fats readily oxidize to release quickly available energy, active persons need and can digest more of these than sedentary persons.

Overeating.—Aside from the previously mentioned mechanical and mental influences, most bodily ills are but manifestations or symptoms of disordered body chemistry. One important factor is overloading the system by overeating. All the food in excess of that necessary to replace waste tissue and supply energy must be thrown off or stored up as fat. The excess puts excessive work on the organs

[6] *The New Health Era*, Hay, 169.

of elimination and clogs the system with unnecessary weight

Hunger.—Remember that hunger is satisfied *in the mouth* and *not* in the stomach. The proof of this is that if you bolt your food you can gorge your stomach almost to bursting and still feel hungry. On the other hand, if you chew each morsel slowly and deliberately until it is so thoroughly mixed with saliva that it is a creamy fluid before it is swallowed involuntarily, your hunger will be satisfied long before your stomach is full. If not especially hungry, skip a meal or two until you are hungry.

Thirst.—Thirst is also satisfied in the mouth. One glass of fluid slowly sipped and rinsed around in the mouth *and relished*, will satisfy your thirst better than several glasses just poured down until your stomach is full, but leaving you still thirsty. These facts are the basis of the paradoxical Hindu aphorism: "Drink solids and chew fluids."

Enjoy Food.—While food, and especially starches, should be chewed to the point of liquid, involuntary swallowing, do not count a certain number of chews to each morsel and thus make eating a boresome task. Definitely and *consciously enjoy your food* by giving your attention to its appetizing appearance and its delightful taste. Do this only while eating and then put it out of mind, so that your mind will not be focussed on your stomach, or on food except while eating or preparing food. If the food is worth eating, it should be worth enjoying. Express this by quietly smacking your lips and saying aloud to your hostess, or to yourself if alone: "Um! How delicious this is!" You thus establish a positive affinity with the pranic essences of your food by your realization and appreciation of them. The combinations should be not only chemically compatible, but they should be pleasing and appetizing to look upon, as well as palatable to the taste.

Do Not Hurry .—Therefore, make your eating and drinking happy functions! Do not allow them to be hurried or rushed through by either bolting your food or gulping your liquids. Many people erroneously feel they have "so much to do," that they have not time to do it. You can do only one thing well at a time. Therefore, *take the time* to do it well. This is most important as regards eating. If you "haven't time to eat" properly, then *do not eat at all*.

No Arguments.—Never allow heated arguments or expressions of irritation, impatience, anger or even resentment, or any negative emotion, to be held, much less expressed, during meals. Such emotions paralyze the digestive system, even to the point of actually stopping the chemical activities of the glands which secrete the digestive juices. Strive to have nothing but happy, constructive conversation, jokes, laughter, etc., at meals.

Giving Thanks.—Since all supply comes from God, to eat without giving thanks is thoughtless ingratitude. Recognizing your dependence upon the Father for food as well as life, tunes you in to His forces. Giving thanks to Him should bring a thrill or a glow of satisfaction and happiness, if through the sincerity of your thanks you make actual contact with His forces.

An Occult Grace.—I am a creator! By the power of my spiritualized will I consciously gather all the forces from this food and use them to manifest health, strength and harmony in all my bodies. And we thank the Father for this manifestation of His bounteous supply. May we use it to His glory in His service. Amen.

Short Thanks.—We thank the Father for this manifestation of His bounteous supply. May we use it to His glory in His service. Amen.

Care.—"Insurance companies have found that even weak and sick people will, if they take good care of themselves, outlive those with robust constitutions who abuse themselves. . . . A young man who a few years ago was scarcely able to drag himself into the sun in Colorado, when he was endeavoring to rid himself of tuberculosis—not only succeeded by dint of following substantially all the rules here laid down, became an athlete and capable of running twenty-five miles for sheer love of sport." [7]

Meat Eatings.—The question of the ethics and morals of meat eating is an individual one which each must decide for himself according to his stage of unfoldment and the degree of transmutation of his atoms. This problem is quite fully dealt with in the chapter on "Thou shalt not kill" in our *The Voice of Isis* and in the chapter on "Transmigration" in our *The Inner Radiance*.

Spiritual Unfoldment.—As we have said before, you should remember that *spiritual unfoldment does not come from the stomach* but from the *heart*. As far as meat being a necessary food is concerned, *The International Food Commission* reports that: "No absolute physiological need exists for meat, since the proteins of meat can be better replaced by other proteins contained in milk, cheese and eggs, as well as by proteins of vegetable origin, such as almonds, pistachios, soy-beans, brazil nuts, pecans and other nuts." [8]

Vegetable Proteins.—"At a recent meeting of the International Council of Physiologists it was decided that meat was not a physiological necessity. It is not thought desirable to fix a minimum meat

---

[7] *How to Live*, Fisher, 160-1.
[8] *Hindu Dietetics*. Sri Sukul, 4.

ration, in view of the fact that *no absolute physiological need for meat exists*, since the proteins of meat can be replaced by other proteins of animal origin, such as those contained in milk; cheese and eggs, as well as by proteins of vegetable origin.'"[9]

The vegetable proteins are also rich in iron, hence are a more valuable source of protein for children and the anemic than is meat.

Starch Digestion.—Since the first stage in the digestion of starch takes place through the action of the enzyme *ptyalin* in the alkaline saliva, it is *absolutely essential* that starchy food be thoroughly chewed for some time—until it is a thick cream—so the *ptyalin* will be thoroughly mixed with it and have time to act, or the starch will ferment when it comes in contact with the acid juices of the stomach which kill the *ptyalin* and stop the digestion of the starch.

Not for Babies.—"Before the teeth are in place, the concentrated starches and cane sugars are never thoroughly split. . . . Introducing starches and sugars before the teeth are developed. . . . is one of the most fertile causes of the frequent fermentations, the bilious attacks, the lack of appetite, the sour vomiting, the eruptions, the irritability, the bedwetting habit, and the general early formation of acid states. . . . by two years of age."[10]

Teeth.—The use of too much soft foods contain-

[9] *How to Live*, Fisher, 40.
[10] *The New Health Era*, Hay, 48, 49.

ing white flour or white sugar, and their acid results, is one of the greatest causes of tooth decay, also of excess acid formation. The Igorots of the Philippines ruin their naturally fine teeth whenever they turn from their coarse diet to our soft, processed foods.

Brush the teeth thoroughly after every meal, especially before going to bed, so particles of food will not decompose and produce acid and promote bacterial growth over night. Brush down and up.

Hard Foods.—Use a considerable amount of hard foods, such as hard toast, stale crusts, grape nuts, nuts and fibrous vegetables which require much chewing. The chewing not only brings out the flavor and increases the relish, but it also exercises the jaws and improves the condition of the teeth and teeth sockets, as well as causes a copious flow of both saliva and gastric juice.

Chew Chew Club.—Therefore, for your teeth's and your health's sake, join the *Chew Chew Club*!

Pyorrhea.—It is said that the only animals besides man that have pyorrhea are the domesticated dog and cat, whose wrong diet is much like man's. In experiments on animals,[11] those deprived of vitamin C gave every symptom of pyorrhea, but liberal use of citrus juices or fruit punch quickly restored them to normal.

---

[11] *Orthodietetics*, Broughton, 54.

Milk.—Raw milk is one of the best of foods, but being a protein it is not digested well with starches or sugars, although cream may be used, as it is a fat. It should be sipped and chewed. The tendency of milk to form mucus can be overcome by the use of fruit juices. Fresh, certified raw milk is recommended, especially for children, as it is alkaline, whereas pasteurized milk is acid.

Goat's Milk.—"Little children, before the end of the second year, need nothing but (mother's) milk. . . . the best substitute is goat's milk. If nothing but pasteurized milk can be obtained, then orange juice should be added to the dairy diet. . . . even for the breast fed infant—Away goes the old familiar bread and milk of our fore-fathers." [12] However, children who are actively exercising, also adults at hard muscular work, can usually oxidize this combination without difficulty.

Sugar.—Refined sugar and candy made therefrom should be avoided. For sweetening, use brown sugar, maple sugar or honey, although rock candy may be used 'between' meals. Sugar should not be used in tea or coffee or with proteins. Dates, figs and raisins may be used freely in place of candy. They are very nutritious and satisfy the taste for sweets.

Weight Reduction.—Heredity and Karma determine the type of body we incarnate in. This cannot

---

[12] *The New Health Era*, Hay, 49-48.

be greatly changed, but it can be kept within shapely proportions by preventing unsightly accumulations of excess fat. One student lost two inches at his waist line in six months by simply omitting bread and cereals from breakfast. Women should not strive for a "boyish figure," but for a well rounded womanly figure. For it is the generous curves which Nature has given their sex which make their figures so attractive, not the immature stringiness of school girls or "pony ballet" girls.

Fat.—Naturally, excess fat comes from excess food, for most stout persons eat three times as much food as is necessary. No "reducing diet" is necessary. Eat all that your appetite demands, but cut out all fat-producing foods. With the cause removed, results follow automatically. Avoid all "fat reducers." They contain dangerous drugs, and are unnecessary if you will follow these directions.

Stop all starches, that is, all white flour products, bread, crackers, macaroni, etc., all cereals, potatoes, rice, etc., if you would reduce.

Stop all sugars, candies and sweet dishes, also all butter, fats and oils.

Omit breakfast entirely or use only grape fruit, oranges or pineapple.

Reducing Diet.—This leaves plenty to eat. Use especially all raw, live vegetable salads, also all cooked vegetables except legumes—dried peas, beans, lentils—and peanuts. Use all fresh fruits except bananas. Ask for canned fruits *without syrup*. On this diet you will have plenty to eat and you can lose a pound or more a day until you get down to the normal weight for your height.

When down to normal you may add a glass of milk, buttermilk or clabber, or an egg yolk beaten up in milk, to your fruit breakfast. You may then also add a moderate amount of meat or fish, if desired, to your main meal, so long as you keep to the compatible combinations.

One Kind.—Do not eat more than one concentrated starch or one protein at a meal. To do so would overbalance the proper proportion you had planned.

Salt.—The less salt used the better. Some authorities report experiments proving it to be a direct cause of high blood pressure.[13] And pepper and hot condiments should be avoided in general, although the Hindus[14] advocate the use of mild sweet spices to flavor many dishes and give variety. The use of celery or vegetable salt is recommended. Use lemon in place of vinegar.

---

[13] *Orthodietetics*, Broughton, 49.
[14] *Hindu Dietetics*, Sukul.

Aluminum.—The older type, and the cheap modern type of aluminum ware should not be used for cooking, as some of the metal is dissolved and is absorbed by the food. This gradually accumulates in the body and causes many gastric and nervous symptoms whose origin is obscure unless it is recognized as aluminum poisoning. The high priced modern ware is made of an aluminum alloy which the makers claim does not give aluminum poisoning. But you can still use your old aluminum ware if you cook everything in patapar paper.

Up to You.—No one can eat your food for you, nor digest it, nor assimilate it, nor excrete its wastes. So the cleansing and rebuilding of your body is *up to you.* And since the matter is under your own control, you have no one to blame but yourself if you are sick.

Putrefaction of Meat.—Some vegetarians claim that meat putrefies in the stomach. Physiologically this is not possible, as the acid and pepsin of the gastric juice digest the meat so quickly that even if putrefying bacteria were present—which is extremely unlikely—they would not have time in which to bring about putrefaction. The symptoms such persons quote as evidence of putrefaction—belching offensive gas etc.—are not those of putrefaction, but of the fermentation produced when starches or sugars are eaten with meat

CHAPTER VI

COMPATIBILITY OF FOODS

Heredity.—Many persons totally disregard the need for proper food combinations. They combine anything that appeals to their taste or appetite, and yet seem healthy and vigorous. They therefore conclude that their way of eating must be correct or they would not feel so well.

This is usually due to the fact that they have inherited a vigorous constitution. And if they are doing hard manual work or taking vigorous outdoor exercise their muscular work will oxidize almost any food. Also the body is so adaptable that it will stand years of abuse and make the best of it

Early Breakdown.—But sooner or later after middle life they have severe illnesses or a "nervous breakdown" and are *suddenly* compelled to "take life easy." The organs which have been so long abused by wrong diet and overwork reach their limit of endurance and rebel. This rebellion may localize as indigestion, diabetes, kidney or heart trouble, high blood pressure, apoplexy, etc. But these are not conditions which have suddenly attacked them.

They are but the focal symptoms and end-results of years of abuse.

Incompatibilities.—The general rule laid down by over thirty years of specific experience and experimentation by Dr. William Howard Hay, and concurred in by many other food specialists who follow along the general line of the school of dietetics founded by him, is that concentrated starches should not be eaten *at the same meal* with either proteins or acid fruits.

Ptyalin.—As we said under Starch Digestion,[1] the action of the enzyme *ptyalin* found in the alkaline saliva begins the digestion of starch into primary sugars, the dextrins and maltose. As this enzyme must be thoroughly incorporated into the starch, chewing the food to a creamy consistency is essential, for the ptyalin can act only in alkaline solution. Although the gastric juice of the stomach is normally slightly acid, when starch is being eaten it reflexly inhibits the acid secretion to a minimum, hence the digestion of the starch can continue for some time in the stomach.

Acid Stimulated.—But when proteins are eaten, they reflexly stimulate the secretion of the acid to a maximum. This immediately stops the further digestion of the starch, which if it has not been thoroughly chewed and insalivated, lies in the

---

[1] Page 53.

stomach and ferments. This produces gas, heartburn, water-brash, excessive acid stomach and toxic accumulations. It is this excess of *acid of fermentation and decomposition*, not the normal acid of secretion, which causes acidosis.

Acidosis.—All the body fluids save four—gastric juice, urine, sweat, vaginal—are alkaline, hence the necessity for 80% alkaline forming food. The amount of acidity is measured by comparing it with the strength of hydrogen ions in water. With water having a formula of pH 7, and normal blood alkalinity represented by pH 7.3 to 7.5 indicating excellent health, a pH of over 7.5 is called hyper-alkalinity or *alkalosis*. Unless excessive, this indicates high functional activity and ample alkaline reserve with which to combat excessive acidity. A pH of less than 7.3 is called hyper-acidity or *acidosis*, and indicates low functional activity.

Symptoms.—A tired feeling, listlessness on awaking, an over-full puffed feeling after meals. Drowsiness, tiring easily, catching cold easily, shortness of breath, skin eruptions, mild eye troubles, pyorrhea, brittle or falling hair, etc. Counteracted by a purge, followed by citrus fruits or fruit punch.

Alkalinity.—The body fluids are kept alkaline by (1) buffer salts—carbonates and phosphates—which resist chemical changes from the normal; by (2) respiration or elimination of carbonic acid gas. Its concentration in the blood regulates the depth of the breathing by affecting the respiratory center in the brain. When the buffer salts and the respiratory system are overtaxed by acid, the body rids itself of the excess acid by (3) excretion through bowels, skin, and chiefly through the kidneys. It is this continual irritation by the acids and toxines that is largely responsible for kidney breakdown (nephritis). All of the above are markedly controlled by (4) diet of compatible foods, largely fruits and vegetables.

Soda.—While alkaline drugs temporarily raise the alkaline reserve, they tend to accumulate in the tissues and are difficult to eliminate, and upset normal acid-alkaline balance. The only natural way to build up a normal alkaline reserve is through a diet in which alkaline-forming foods predominate over acid-forming foods in a ratio of 80 to 20.

Proteins.—Proteins demand an acid medium and pepsin for their digestion, hence are digested in the stomach, where those very conditions prevent the digestion of starches.

Rules.—The rules generally agreed upon by the new Compatibility School of dietetics are as follows :

1. Do *not* combine *proteins*—(meats, fish, egg whites, milk, cheese and nuts) with concentrated starches—(breakfast foods, rice, potatoes, ripe dried beans or peas, macaroni, spaghetti, noodles, bread,

crackers, cake, pastry or other white flour products). Any of the non-starch vegetables may be combined with the proteins.

2. Do *not* combine *proteins* with sweets, except maple sugar and honey, unheated preferred. Tupola honey is recommended for its high percentage of levulose or predigested sugar.

3. Do *not* combine *starches* with acid fruits.

4. Starches may be combined with any vegetables and with sweets.

5. Proteins combine with all vegetables and fruits and fruit juices, except the concentrated starches.

You can use much the same foods you usually do when in the right combination.

All vegetables contain some starch, but they are classed as starches—that is, concentrated starches— only when they contain 40% or more of starch.

Doctors Untrained.—Some doctors scoff at this classification, but doctors as a class are abysmally ignorant as to diet, more so than the average good cook, *unless* they have made a special study of it. And even then they lack a correct understanding *unless* they have studied it not merely from the stand-point of calories and vitamins, but from the standpoint of the *chemical end-products of digestion in combination.* The reason for this ignorance is that most medical schools give an average of only six hours' instruction on diet during four years study! (About as much as they give to nursing.) And most of that miserly six hours is given over to statistics as to calories, vitamins, etc. and how to prepare junket, koomiss and other "delicacies" to "tempt the appetite" of the patient who usually should be fasting!

Experience.—On the contrary Dr. Hay, and those who follow the general reforms introduced by him, by repeated *chemical analysis of stomach contents* at various stages, and by *years of clinical experience* in curing thousands of chronic cases—indigestion, catarrh, rheumatism, arthritis, kidney, bladder, liver, sinus trouble, asthma, hay fever, gall bladder, skin diseases, etc.,—many of whom had been months in hospitals and sanitariums and had been given up as hopeless, has *definitely proved* that the above rules are not mere theory or fad but are laws. For those who follow them are cured.

Eating Habits.—The principal change this diet will make in your eating habits is that if you have a cereal and toast or bread for breakfast, you should not have acid fruit juices, meat or egg whites or else such juices should be taken an hour before breakfast. Egg yolks and bacon are classed as fats and can be used with cereals or starches. If you do not have any starch at breakfast, then the citrus fruits may be taken with it. Orange and milk make an ideal breakfast.

For lunch and dinner you will soon get used to eliminating bread, potatoes, rice, noodles, etc. when meat, fish or other proteins are used. But when plenty of other vegetables are used with proteins, you will soon become accustomed to the absence of starch. If you wish one starch meal a day, using potatoes, rice, macaroni, etc., have all you want at a meal, when proteins and acid fruits are not used. But do not use more than one concentrated starch in the meal. You do not need to skimp your meals, especially when changing to the new diet, as there is a great variety of foods to use.[1] It is the proper selection *and combination* that is important.

Processed Foods.—It is best to avoid most processed and devitalized foods, such as prepared breakfast foods, etc. unless specially irradiated with ultra-violet rays. Citrus fruits should be eaten at least an hour before a cereal or starch meal.

Bran.—Foods with more than the natural amount of bran found in grains should be avoided. Bran should not be eaten alone. Its action is due to its irritation of the intestines, and its continued use often causes grave bowel troubles, even becoming embedded in its walls and having to be scraped out. Its sharp edges are said even to amputate the minute villi of the intestine, which absorb the food.

---

[1] Use freely of fresh vegetables and fruits in their seasons, and omit old winter potatoes and roots, dried beans, dried fruits, old nuts etc. when the fresh ones are in the market.

CHAPTER VII

COOKING

Raw Foods.—As a general rule, eat as much live, raw foods as possible. Raw foods are called "live foods" because they have not been killed nor their prana altered by cooking. They still retain much of their living prana and magnetism unless they are stale. They digest more easily than when cooked, and they pass through the system more rapidly, hence there is little time for fermentation or decomposition, therefore no formation of toxic poisons.

In general, do not cook any food which Nature has made palatable when raw. This includes salads, fruits, nuts, raisins, figs, dates and other dried fruits, berries, celery, carrots, beets, cabbage, cucumbers, tomatoes, radishes, grapes, onions, green peppers, cauliflower, asparagus etc. It also includes butter, cheese, milk, cream, sour milk, buttermilk, honey, olive and other vegetable oils. All raw foods should be well washed to remove as far as possible the poisons with which they may have been sprayed.

Cooking.—Baking, broiling or steaming are the best methods of cooking.

Cooking destroys some vitamins,[1] and boiling also

---

[1] See advertising pages for our booklet on *Vitamins*.

dissolves out many essential minerals which are usually poured down the sink. A teaspoonful of powdered kelp a day is recommended by some to replace many of the lost vitamins and minerals.

Most starchy foods, cereals and unripe fruit should be thoroughly cooked before eating.

Vegetables.—Most vegetables should be cooked (steamed) with little or no water. Where water is used, it dissolves out of the vegetables many vitamins and minerals. If it cannot all be cooked down and absorbed by the vegetables, it should be saved to use in gravy or as a juice-drink with or between meals.

Patapar Paper.—Vegetables are best cooked by washing without paring, and tied up in "patapar paper"[1] and placed in a small amount of boiling water. This, preserves all their flavors, juices, vitamins and minerals. And there is no comparison in their flavor. Once eaten cooked in patapar paper, you will never cook them any other way. The paper can be obtained, at any ten-cent store, and can be washed and used again and again.

Vitamins.—There is little need to go into the complicated subject of specific vitamins and the twelve mineral salts needed by the body. If the wide range of diet, recommended herein, especially the raw foods, is followed, you will obtain all the vitamins and minerals in generous amounts.

---

[1] In England called "Cropar paper" instead of "Patapar."

Roast.—Use two long spoons for turning a roast. A fork pierces the surface and allows the juices to escape.

Tins.—If you use muffin or other tins for baking tomatoes, apples, stuffed peppers, onions, etc., they will keep their shape better.

Potassium.—Potassium is of especial importance in neutralizing acids, preventing and eliminating calcium deposits which are a feature of the degenerative diseases; in eliminating abnormal growths, ulcers, rheumatic and gouty and old-age symptoms, and in toning up the skin. As it is easily eliminated from the body many persons suffer to some degree from potassium deficiency. While all salad greens and vegetables grown above the ground are generally rich in potassium, in addition to their use we recommend as especially important the frequent use of potassium broth at least two or three times a week. A quantity can be made once or twice a week and kept in a closed jar in the refrigerator ready for use as needed.

Potassium broth is made as follows:

Into two quarts water put:

1 lb. Celery (3 cups when finely shredded or cut)
1 lb. Carrots " "   "   "   "   " "
¼ lb. Spinach (1 cup when "   "   " "
1 oz. Parsley (¼ cup when "   "   " "

Vegetable salt to taste (about one level tablespoon for this amount.)

The vegetables may be put through a food chopper or finely cut or shredded. When shredded or cut vegetables are used, the broth will have a very delicate flavor and will be clearer in color. There is no objection, however, to the fine particles of vegetable matter which will be found remaining in the broth after it has been strained when ground vegetables are used in the preparation.

The cooking time is most important in the preparation of this broth. The vegetables should be put in cold water and brought to a boil slowly—in about twenty minutes. After the boiling point is reached, the broth should be allowed to simmer for from five to ten minutes. Five minutes is sufficient if the vegetables have been ground. Eight to ten minutes if cut or shredded.

CHAPTER VIII

VARIOUS SUGGESTIONS

Eyes.—According to the elaborate experiments of Dr. W. H. Bates[1] and the school who follow him, nearly all eye defects are due to unconscious nervous strain which affects the muscles of accommodation and so disturbs the lens of the eye. This applies to squints, divergent vision and crossed eyes, as well as to accommodation. Since perfect darkness relaxes the tension, his remedy, which he calls "palming," is to place the crossed palms of the hands gently over the eyes in such a way as to exclude all light, but without touching the eyeballs. Since we see or interpret our vision with our minds and not with the eyes, thought and memory play an important part in correcting our vision.

Palming.—With your palms over the eyes, think of the blackest things you know of. Remember how intensely black an automobile is or black cloth, especially black velvet, and mentally shift from one black object to another. Pin a very black advertise-

---

[1] For details see *The Cure of Imperfect Sight by treatment without glasses*, Bates.

ment on the wall a few feet away and see how much of the finer print you can read without strain. Then try "palming" and "thinking black" a minute or two and then see how much better you can read the finer print. Then look away at some distant object, but without strain. This also relaxes the eyes. These are very simple exercises, but are of the utmost importance, and if persisted in will cure almost all eye defects.

Blinking.—Blinking the eyes gently but rapidly, also swinging the eyes from side to side and diagonally upward and downward, also closing the eyes tightly and opening them widely, tones and strengthens all the muscles of the eyes. But palming and ''thinking black" and testing your eyes with an advertisement or chart is the most important factor.

Practice reading without glasses for a few minutes. Do the best you can without strain. When the letters blur, rest the eyes by palming, and repeat many times during the day. Palm and blink and focus on distant objects, especially green fields or trees, many times during the day.

Practice palming and blinking during moving pictures or while reading on moving trains.

Boric Acid.—If the eyes are inflamed, rinse them in a solution of boric add.

Do not read in a waning light or in the bright sunlight, or with lamplight directly in front of you.

Have the light over your shoulder or at least at the side, at the left if writing.

Detoxification and correct diet will also help the eyes.

Sleep.—Sleep is Nature's greatest restorative, for during sound sleep we withdraw completely from the physical body and ascend into the higher realms where our astral body becomes more or less completely re-charged with the pranic life-force. This we bring back with us to recharge our physical body. During sleep is when we assimilate most of our food, grow and make repairs. Some who are psychic sometimes return quite tired or depleted. This is because they have indulged in too strenuous activities in the astral world. Make up your mind that, as a rule, you go to sleep to rest and recuperate, and not to work in the astral; your real work and lessons are here on the physical plane. That is why you incarnated here. Five or six hours sleep should be enough when properly detoxicated, although some mental workers need seven or eight.

Insomnia.—Insomnia is usually due to acid fer-mentation in the small intestine. The treatment is to counteract that acidity as quickly as possible. Therefore, if nervous, wakeful and sleepless, take a full glass of grapefruit juice.[1] Also take a high enema with lukewarm water only, hot water being too stimulating.

---

[1] Just before going to bed.

Also take the *Calming* or the *Cleansing Breath*. Also use the *Prayer to the Divine Indweller*, or to the loving I Am Presence, and let Him bear all your burdens and anxieties. Then drop off to sleep in calm confidence in His love.

Protective Invocation.—If disturbed by astral forces or entities, take the drink and enema first, then use the above mentioned prayer or our *Protecting Invocation* and rely upon die protection of the blazing white Christ-light with which it surrounds you. If these psychic disturbances occur frequently, it sometimes helps to crush some gum camphor and cloves together and keep them in a closed jar during the day, but open it in your bedroom during the night. Undeveloped entities do not like these odors.

Some sensitive persons sleep better with the head toward the North, but this is not important.

Alcohol.—As we have explained elsewhere,[2] alcohol and narcotics disintegrate the astral sheaths which protect your psychic centers from invasion by astral forces which may lead to obsession. Hence the frequent use of alcoholic beverages should be positively refused by those who seriously desire spiritual advancement and mastery.

"Special classes of workmen have been tested as to their efficiency under liquor in small amounts and without it entirely, and it was *invariably found* that

---

[2] *The Voice of Isis*, Curtiss, 100.

the liquor was a handicap, altho invariably the workmen *thought* they could work harder by its aid. Alcohol, numbs the sense of fatigue and so deceives the user. . . . People who indulge in alcohol show less resistance to infectious diseases than abstemious individuals."[3]

Tobacco.—"Tobacco although classed as a narcotic does not contain the elements so destructive to the psychic centers, in fact, when not used to excess, is rather soothing. It does, however, injuriously affect the heart and nervous system. From an occult standpoint one of the greatest objections to its use is its tendency to form a habit. It goes without saying that the aspirant for the spiritual life must be master of all conditions and functions and a slave to none." [4], "Prof. Pack, of the University of Utah, finds that tobacco-using athletes are distinctly inferior to those who abstain. . . . There is also much experimental evidence to show that tobacco induces arterial changes."[3] Tobacco is especially harmful to women because of their more sensitive nervous system. Their nervous and excitable conditions usually have a basis of acidosis and toxemia, hence should be soothed by detoxication instead of by tobacco.

Vaccination.—"Those nations most thoroughly

---

[3] *How to Live*, Fisher, 81, 82.
[4] *The Voice of Isis*, Curtiss, 101.

vaccinated, as the Philippine Islands, Japan and Italy, have today the highest incidence and *highest mortality* from smallpox of all nations, while those nations that do not observe the rite of vaccination are lowest in both morbidity and mortality. If vaccination prevents small-pox, then those nations enforcing vaccination should be free from the plague. . . . Yet the opposite is true, as anyone can prove by consulting the vital statistics of every civilized country keeping health records." [5]

Serums.—Aside from their uncertainty and often disastrous after effects, we should not wilfully pollute our blood stream with the blood or serum from the animal kingdom, still less with either disease germs themselves or their products. With detoxication and proper diet their uncertain aid will not be needed.

Surgery.—Surgery is seldom justified in dis-eased conditions, as in most cases *it does not remove the cause* of the trouble, only the result, namely, the diseased part or organ. "Dr. Charles Mayo (of the great Mayo surgical clinic) said a few years ago that nine-tenths of the internal surgical operations of today never should have been done. . . . it is the writer's firm conviction that ninety-nine percent of all internal operations performed today never should

---

[5] *The New Health Era*, Hay, 175.

have been done."[6] Dr. John B. Dever, Professor of Surgery at the University of Pennsylvania, stated some years ago that the records of his thousands of operations showed that only about 13% were of any permanent benefit.

Tonsils.—"No tonsil is ever so hopelessly diseased as to deserve removal, and one of the largest and best equipped pathological laboratories in this country reports that in *one thousand tonsils removed. . . .* examination showed that but 7% were diseased."[7]

Specialists.—Specialists are trained to deal with certain particular organs or conditions. They spend much time on diagnosis and their diagnosis may be wonderful, but their treatment is often only palliative. It is not the organ or part that needs treatment, but the underlying bodily conditions (chemistry) which permit the symptoms to appear in a particular part.

Doctors.—From the above remarks, it might seem that we were opposed to doctors or belittle their services. Far from it. We recognize that thousands of noble men are devoting their whole lives to relieving suffering humanity. What we wish to emphasize is that most of their services would not be needed if the basic factors—acidosis, toxemia, de-

---

[6] *The New Health Era*, Hay, 22.
[7] *The New Health Era*, Hay, 28.

structive thoughts and emotions—which either cause most diseases or permit them to manifest, were eliminated. To teach you how to eliminate these *causes* is the object of this volume.

Radionics.—One of the most important steps in modern medical practice is the development of the use of high frequency radio waves in the treatment of diseased conditions, especially of cancer. The instruments using such radio tubes are able to diagnose the condition by its vibratory wave-length, and to charge the patient's body with the wave-length which will neutralize the diseased condition and cause complete recovery in an amazingly short time. But to remain relieved or cured, the patient must, of course, *change his habits of life*, as herein outlined, which caused the condition.

Wherever such radionic instruments can be found in the hands of competent practitioners, such as our own staff, we recommend that you be treated by them for serious ailments. The one known as the "Radioclast" is the most specific in diagnosis and treatment of all we have seen. It is not necessary for the patient to be present to receive an accurate diagnosis, for with this instrument a complete diagnosis can be made from a few drops of the patient's blood sent on a piece of clean white blotter or cotton wool.[8]

---

[8] Write the author if interested in such a diagnosis.

CHAPTER IX

MENTAL INFLUENCES

Your health results from a divine harmony of body, mind and spirit, *i. e.*, a pure body, a tranquil mind and a Soul stayed on God.

Mind Soars.—"'As a man thinketh in his heart, so is he,' is more than a trite saying, for it is capable of active and most convincing proof. As the body clears of waste material with which it was formerly loaded, the mind soars to heights not formerly glimpsed by toxic minds, and new worlds seem to open".[1]

Origin of Thought.—While thought originates in the mind in the mental world outside of and above the body, it must utilize the body and its functions to express itself on earth. And this expression depends upon the condition of the body as an instrument. Slow thinking, poor reasoning power, loss of memory, lack of the power to concentrate are all evidence, not of a defective brain, but of toxemia. Usually nothing is wrong with the brain, but its functioning is interfered with by the toxic character of the blood supplied to it.

---

[1] *The New Health Era*, Hay, 162.

Emotions.—Just as inharmonious, depressed and toxic conditions of the body have a corresponding influence on the mind, so does your mind, and especially your emotions, have an enormous effect upon the body. A mental shock may cause fainting. Worry interferes with both digestion and sleep, etc.

Mental Health.—As we have already said: "Mental health is the result of right thinking. Therefore, we must learn so to *order our thoughts* that they shall be constructive and helpful. We must also study the laws of mind so that we may work in harmony with them and not waste our mental forces, in vain imaginings, or fritter them away in worry, etc. . . . . We must *train our minds* to work in harmony with our ideals and principles of life, and it will then radiate harmony and health." [2]

Role of Mind.—"It is often ignorantly said that all ills of the body are caused by the mind. This, of course, is obviously untrue, for all physical injuries, external and internal poisonings, psychic disorders, and all disorders resulting from improper diet, are not caused by the mind; they come from without. *But all the sensations and symptoms of illness* are experienced through the reaction of the mind to the inharmonious cause of the sensation." [2] Hence instead of ignoring the body and trying to counteract the effects of its broken laws by the mind and higher

---

[2] *The Message of Aquaria*, Curtiss, 151-51-52.

powers, the first thing to do is to see that you do not poison the blood which bathes the whole body, especially the brain and nervous systems, with the results of perverted body chemistry and uneliminated wastes. A brain so nourished cannot act normally. A thorough cleansing of the body will not only change the chemical condition of your blood and tissues, but will also change your mental reactions and your whole psychology.

Mental Harmony.—When harmonized, the mind, yields to the normal needs of a pure body without being hampered by grossness. Yet it controls the body's desires without over-indulging them.

When inharmonious, both body and mind derange each other by confusion of elements, which wastes the force of each.

Thought a Magnet.—Thought is a magnet. It attracts to you others' thoughts of like character which tend to find expression through you, unless counteracted by an opposite thought of greater power.

Subconscious Mind.—Especially do your emotions have an enormous effect. All negative emotions have a most devitalizing and disintegrating, in some cases an *actually poisonous*, effect upon the body. This is due to their effect upon the subconscious mind, which controls all the functions of life—circulation, respiration, digestion, assimilation, excretion, repair and chemical activities—through the solar plexus and the sympathetic nervous system.

Governs Body.—"But the subconscious mind must not be thought of as merely the janitor in the basement who supplies the furnace with fuel and removes the ashes, for it is far more. It is an aspect of mind which governs all our reflex activities or unconscious and instinctive reactions, and these functions are by no means entirely automatic. In addition to this, under normal conditions it suggests or gives us a craving for *what we should eat*, what we should wear and how we should protect and take care of our body through diet, exercise, recreation, etc., even if these suggestions are overruled by our preconceived, environmental and family ideas, by our vanity, our indolence, or the ideas of others which we impose upon it. If we learned to follow the guidance of the subconscious *as to the welfare of the body*, we would seldom be sick or get rundown and stagnant. Yet this instinctive mind must not be given full and unlimited sway, for it also expresses the passions, desires and appetites of the animal body which must be checked, governed and directed by the two higher aspects of the mind which are above it and which are responsible for the degree to which it is indulged."[3]

---

[3] Send for a copy of this article *Regeneration and the Mind*, Curtiss.

Mental Laws.—As we have said elsewhere: "Remember that one of the fundamental laws of mind is: Every thought tends to express itself in action unless counteracted or neutralized by an opposite thought of greater power. Therefore, we must *refuse to think* the kind of thoughts that we do not wish expressed through us. But never fight them; for to do so we are concentrating upon them and giving them greater power. Instead of resisting or fighting them, we must simply *turn our minds away* from them by concentrating on and filling our minds with the opposite kind of thoughts, ones which we do wish to have expressed through us.

Power Over You.—"Another fundamental law is: Every thought that we admit into our minds and contemplate we give a power over us. But *we do not have to admit* into our minds, contemplate and go over and over every thought that may arise in or be presented to our consciousness. We can turn away from and refuse to dwell upon those thoughts which do not measure up to the ideals of our lives. Therefore, remember that we do not have to admit or contemplate thoughts of evil or ill health *unless we choose* to do so. The supreme importance of carefully choosing and controlling our thoughts as the basis of our lives lies in the fact that every word and act is but the ultimate expression of a thought or instinct. Good thoughts beget good words and acts, and vice versa, and all have their reflex action in the body.

Suggestion.—"The great significance of these laws lies in the fact that our subconscious mind is extremely suggestible. It is possible to be made actually ill by being continually told how ill you look. And you can greatly encourage and help others by telling them how much better and happier they are looking today.

Do Not Accept.—"You do not have to respond to suggestions, unless you deliberately choose to do so, if you keep your mind poised, discriminating and positive.

Flesh Responds.—"Any positive idea or thought held in the rational mind acts like a command which the subconscious mind takes up and endeavors to express in action, in function and even in structure; that is, it endeavors to build the logical meaning of that thought into our very flesh. This is why we ultimately come to express in our looks and acts the predominating type of thoughts which we think, *i. e.*, gluttonous, selfish, vain, crafty, cruel, etc., or pure, frank, kind and sympathetic.

Repercussion.—"If the power of the mind to actually *alter the structure of the body* is so great that by the continued morbid concentration on the five wounds of Jesus, the stigmata—the actual physical wounds in the hands, feet and side—appeared on the body of St Francis of Assissi and several other medieval psychics, as well as upon the body of the young peasant girl, Theresa Neuman of Komersreuth, Austria, who for over four years (1926-30) was under the investigation of the greatest physicians, scientists and psychic researchers of Europe, what a mighty regeneration of the body can not the mind accomplish if repeatedly focussed with equally intense concentration upon the manifestation in our flesh of the divine perfection—the Divine Life, health, love, power and happiness—of the Divine Indweller, if we will only strive to live in His consciousness and in the realization of His indwelling presence.

Rebuilding.—"All the cells of every tissue and organ of the body are continually dividing and growing and producing new cells to replace the cells that are worn out by each day's activities. Some tissues are replaced more rapidly than other more dense ones, such as the bones, but science estimates that at the end of every seven years we have an entirely new body which contains not a single cell we had seven years before. And it is upon these sensitive new cells thus constantly formed that the subconscious mind impresses the characteristics of the thoughts we habitually hold or hold temporarily but, under great emotional stress or concentration. Thus we are constantly changing the make-up of our body by the character of the thoughts we hold.

Regeneration.—"This law is the key-note of regeneration; for if we hold the idea that we must sometimes be sick, must ultimately grow old, have our body wear out and die, quite naturally those fixed and stagnant ideas are built into and manifest in our flesh and so stagnate all our vital functions, and old age and death necessarily follow. We, therefore, have to withdraw from the physical world because the functions of our instrument of manifestation have become so stagnant that the life-force from the higher worlds can no longer flow through them.

Reincarnation.—"This is the reason for reincarnation. We must keep returning again and again until we learn to live in and be dominated, *not by the subconscious mind* of the body which is mortal, nor by the consciousness of the rational mind which is limited in expression, but by the Super-conscious Mind of the Higher Self or Divine Indweller who is immortal. We must reincarnate until we can build up and perfect a body that will express the Real or Spiritual Self instead of merely that manifested fragment of that Self which we call the human personality or personal self. But, as the Lord said to Job:[4] 'If there be an interpreter (the illumined mind) to shew unto man his uprightness (or divine perfection); then. . . . his flesh shall be fresher

---

[4] Job, xxxiii, 23-5.

than a child's; he shall return to the days of his youth.'"[5]

Mental Attitude.—You must have a positive desire to recover. A mere weak wish to be relieved of suffering is not enough. There must be a positive desire, a burning resolution that is not only willing to "take the trouble" to *change your habits of life*, in spite of the opinions of those who do not understand your reasons. And there must be a determined *will to carry it through* to success, to joyous radiant health. Defeat is deadly. Never accept it.

Irish.—It is said that an Irishman is never down, except to get a better hold. Then you should be Irish in this sense. Never give up, but always be looking for a better hold.

Planetary Conditions.—Astrological conditions undoubtedly affect the health. But astrology teaches you to "Rule your stars" and not give way to their forces as though they were fate. If the body is kept detoxicated and alkaline, and the mind kept positive and responsive to constructive forces only, any adverse astrological conditions can be neutralized or turned into constructive channels, just as the sailor adjusts his sails to make adverse winds push him onward to his port.

---

[5] See lesson *Regeneration and the Mind*, Curtiss.

CHAPTER X

EMOTIONS

Your emotions have an even more powerful effect upon the body than do your thoughts, as they act directly upon the emotional or astral body and thus repercus or react upon the physical.

Constructive Emotions.—Joy and happiness bring smiles and stimulate all the bodily functions and give a general sense of well-being. Love suffuses the body with a warm constructive glow, while prayer and spiritual aspiration tune your mind into the uplifting vibrations of the spiritual world, and your body responds in harmony and health.

Negative Emotions.—On the other hand, negative emotions have a decidedly disintegrating, and in many cases an actually poisonous, effect.

Fear.[1]—Fear paralyzes not only your muscles, so that you may literally be "scared stiff," but it also paralyzes all the digestive functions, so that food in the stomach lies like a dead weight. It may also paralyze the sphincter muscles so they cannot retain the body wastes. But since you are not a mortal,

---

[1] Send for free copy of lesson *Fear Not*, Curtiss. Also see *Psalms*, xci, 5 and 7.

but an immortal, spiritual being, there is nothing to fear if you rely confidently and absolutely on that inner Spiritual Self or I Am Presence which is your Real Self, for guidance and protection.

Fear is bred of ignorance or misunderstanding, and causes worry over health or other conditions, thus depleting the vitality. According to Dr. Hay it is evidence of devitalization due to toxemia.[2]

Disease and Old Age.—"Do you fear disease, or even catching cold? If so, that fear paralyzes your natural immunity, lowers your vitality and aids in bringing the disease upon you. For fear causes weakness, disintegration and hence weak spots, and the weak spots ultimately break down and make gaps which let the evil forces enter. The debilitating effects of fear also cause sluggish functioning of your organs and inability to produce their normal secretions.

"Do you fear old age? Such fear generates the negative thought-pictures of old age, and you naturally begin to react to them, whereas had you realized that old age can be mellow, gracious, wise, beloved and beautiful, you would be reacting to those constructive thought-pictures instead of to the negative, and would forget the years.

"Mere recognition of evil for what it is—a mortal-created negative and disintegrating center of force

---

[2] *The New Health Era*, Hay, 113.

—does not necessarily involve fear of it or contamination by it. You are contaminated by it only to the extent that you respond to and give it power over you. And *you do not have to respond*. But if you refuse to recognize mud in the gutter and do not step over or go around it, you may be besmirched by it."[3]

Timid Souls.—Timid souls become so negative that they fear everything new; fear the opinions of their friends and all the dire predictions of the neighbors, etc. This can be overcome by taking a positive stand for the truths and laws you have learned—the laws of health for instance—and prove your sincerity by following them out.

Over 99% of anticipated fears are groundless, hence useless.

Anger.—Anger is so extremely destructive an emotion that it generates poisons in such quantities that they can be chemically detected in the blood.[4] The milk of nursing mothers has been so poisoned by fits of anger that their babies died. It raises the blood pressure and literally makes you "hot under the collar." The saying, "I was so mad I could die," has literally come true in many cases. There-

---

[3] See lesson *Fear Not*. Curtiss.

[4] It is claimed by some that if a person who has been furiously angry can be induced shortly afterward to breathe into a chilled tumbler or bottle, a few drops of moisture from his breath will condense inside the cold vessel. If this liquid is placed on the tongue of a cat, it will soon show signs of poisoning according to the size of the dose.

fore, immediately check any tendency to irritable expressions which may lead to anger. Irritableness usually has its basis in toxemia and should at once suggest a purge. Even resentment is disintegrating.

Resentment.—One student wrote us: "I have been very nervous for many years and have developed diabetes. Also I *hold resentment* against one who should be my support and help but who has held me back every step of the way." We replied: "The basis of your nervous condition and organic inharmonies is largely a mental one, due to the fact that you hold resentment. A careful study of our lesson *Judge Not*, will show you that resentment is a very disintegrating force. And since you receive back the return current from everything you send out, you have been *devitalising yourself* by every wave of resentment you have sent out, as it returns to the sender. No wonder you feel the possibility of sudden illness or death; for you have been generating the forces which produce just such conditions, and are being warned against them from within. Therefore, you cannot expect full freedom from nervousness, fear of death or from your physical illness as long as you continue to send out the disintegrating forces of resentment and the paralyzing force of fear."

"Never mind what anyone has done to you. That is past and gone, and will be taken care of by karmic law in due season. It is holding on to it that holds you back. Realize that no one can hold you back but yourself, unless you are so negative and lacking in courage quietly to assert your rights that *you permit it*. Remember that you must forget as well as forgive; for as long as you are holding on to the memory of the condition and your resentment, you have not really forgiven." [5]

Jealousy.—Jealousy and envy are acidifying and corroding forces similar to rust, but more virulent. "If we analyze our motives when inclined to speak critically of others, we will usually find an element of pride, envy, jealousy, fear or a desire to triumph or feel superior to the one criticized. The Real Self of us is never critical, is never envious of the possessions of others; for we have incarnated with possessions of our own. The things in our environment are just those needed for our training and unfoldment. . . . Our Real Self is never jealous of the attainments of others, for we incarnated to *manifest our own* attainments, faculties and qualities which we gained in the past. Hence, instead of resenting the success of others we should rejoice in it, as they should in ours." [5]

Laughter.—"Laugh and grow fat" is an old adage that expresses a great truth. For all the constructive emotions relax nervous tension and

---

[5] Send for free copy of lesson *Judge Not*, Curtiss.

inhibitions, and stimulate all glandular activities, equalize the circulation and promote assimilation and repair.

No Controversies.—The hostess unconsciously recognizes this law when she is careful to select only guests who will harmonize. For the same reason controversial subjects and arguments are banned, for any inharmony or mental clashing will ruin the digestion of the most compatible foods, while jokes, laughter and merriment will help digest even the most incompatible combination—*but* it will not neutralize their harmful end-products. (See also page 50.)

Your Reactions.—Remember it is not things, people and conditions which make you suffer, but *your reaction* to them. And that reaction *you can control* by a positive attitude of mind, and a realization that through the power of the I Am Presence within, you are the master of them.

"Realize that it is not your tasks or duties that worry you or retard your evolution, but *your attitude of mind* toward them, the permitting of everyday trifles so to occupy your mind that you never let them go.

Joys.—"Joyful news makes the heart glad and refreshes the body. The little joys of life are just as satisfying as the little cares are annoying. While you are facing the little cares, watch out for the little joys. . . . If you dwell in the little joys, they run together and soon break out into a mighty soul-satisfying happiness which will be like a strong, deep undercurrent of joy bearing you through all the cares and sorrows of life."[6]

Change.—"The law of change is the law of life, and applies to peoples, civilizations, customs, ideas and religions, as well as to physical forms. . . . Change is essential to all growth and progress, even the change of disintegration—whether of old forms, customs, habits or thoughts—that new and better types may manifest."

You also need a change of environment. A vacation or frequent little outings, even a walk through the park, change the vibrations of your aura and your attitude of mind. They enable you to make new contacts and arouse new interests in life, thus contributing constructive ideas, sensations, as well as exercise, to the benefit of your health.

Recreation.—Your changes should be constructive and fun and joy producing. If so, they are recreating. But they must he wisely planned to include ample rest and relaxation. Many plan so many activities on their vacations that they come home all tired out. Make your re-creation the dominant factor in all your changes.

Overwork.—The man who "breaks down," or

---

[6] *The Voice of Isis*, Curtiss, 36, 5, 53.

has so-called neurasthenia, in middle life, and the college student who thinks he has ruined his health by "over study" and who are benefited by a vacation, are both suffering from bad habits of life. Chief of these is acidosis and toxemia from wrong diet. A course of acid and toxic elimination, with its attendant relief of mental strain, will usually cure such breakdowns in a few days.

Periodic Depression.—Many women suffer periodic depression in connection with their monthly cycle, but if they will take a one day purge and fast, just, before the period, followed by a low-protein diet, all trouble can usually be eliminated. This also applies to disorders of the climateric period.

Optimism.—It is not only your birthright, but your *duty to others* to be happy. Keeping the body free from abnormal products and accumulations will make your body so healthy that, you will naturally be happy. But you should also keep a positive and harmonious attitude toward life. Realize that seldom is anything so bad that it couldn't be worse. Give thanks then that things are no worse than they are, and go resolutely, positively and cheerfully about remedying them.

Determination.—The sun will rise every day, whether you see it or not, and it will continue to rise every day until the end of time. Each day is a new day, a new incarnation. The old is past and gone and need not be lived over, even in thought. Each day is a *new opportunity* for you to demonstrate the degree of your growth, the degree of your realization of the Law, and the amount of your courage and determination.

Smile.—Therefore, make a practice of greeting every *person* and also every *condition* with a smile, and radiate your positive determination to conquer harmoniously.

Animal Emotions.—Remember that all negative and destructive emotions such as fear, anger, hatred, resentment, jealousy, envy, greed etc.—*are not your emotions*, but those of the animal self. They well up from the subconscious mind, and if you allow them to express they make you react like an animal instead of like a spiritual being. And you must pay the penalty for giving them expression by reaping the results of their effects upon your body, mind and spirit.

Remember also that *you do not have to respond* to and give them expression.

All the harmonious and constructive emotions—such as joy, happiness, love, compassion, pity, unselfishness, self-sacrifice etc.—come not from the animal self, but from the Divine Self. Hence these emotions *should be deliberately cultivated* and given constant expression until their expression becomes instinctive and habitual. See the next chapter for directions.

CHAPTER XI

SPIRITUAL INFLUENCES

"Know ye not that ye are the temple of God, and that the Spirit of God dwelleth in you?. . . . for the temple of God is holy, which temple ye are."

I Corinthians, iii, 16, 17.

"Come, O Lord of Life and Love and Beauty, Thou who art myself and yet are God, and dwell in this body of flesh, radiating all the beauty of holiness and perfection, that the flesh may out-picture all that Thou art within."

Prayers of the O. C. M., Curtiss, 6.

While in this short treatise we cannot go into detail, we may say that healing from the higher realms falls into three general groups: *Psychic healing* or that performed by the aid of discarnate doctors and groups of specially trained helpers in the astral world; *Faith healing*, or that performed by prayer and faith; *Spiritual healing*, or that performed by direct invocation of angelic and cosmic forces.

Psychic Induction.—"Many sensitive persons soon develop symptoms of the malady with which a deceased loved one passed out. Such persons suffer just as acutely as though they really had such a physical disease. . . . Such persons are simply suffering from astral conditions unwittingly thrown over them through magnetic induction by the deceased loved one who is trying to make them recognize him. . . . This frequently ceases or is 'cured' when they recognize its source. If it is not, it should be stopped by repeatedly challenging the departed one and demanding that he withdraw from their aura and remain outside it in the future." [1] Many cases of "instant healing" are of this type, for there is no pathological or structural change to be corrected,—only the astral influence to be removed.

Psychic Healing.—True psychic healing is accomplished either by independent healers, often American Indians, usually medicine men, for they are in close rapport with Nature-forces and are able to direct them to great advantage; by deceased physicians and their helpers, or by bands of trained workers under some higher Teacher. The hundreds of seemingly miraculous cures accomplished by the celebrated deceased English physician, Dr. Beal, through the mediumship of Miss E. M. Harvey, are strikingly described in her three books, *The House of Wonder*, *One Thing I Know*, and *Dr. Beal*. Similar marvelous healings by bands of trained deceased persons are continually accomplished by "The Guild of Spiritual Healing," under the leadership of "Dr. Lascelles" of London. These are only two ex-

---

[1] For further details see *Realms of the Living Dead*, Curtiss, 89, 90.

amples of many, many other psychic sincere healing circles in all parts of the world.

Invisible Helpers. Similar miraculous healings, also other marvelous answers to prayer, are daily being performed by the Order's band of Invisible Helpers under the leadership of Harriette Augusta Curtiss, with the technical assistance of Dr. D. Hayes Agnew, former professor of Surgery at the University of Pennsylvania, and the Masters who are back of the Order of Christian Mystics. Many of these marvelous cures have been reported in our *News Letters* for over twenty years.

Noon Prayer Service.—Every day at noon a "Prayer of Demonstration Service" is held in the Sanctuary at the Headquarters of the Order of Christian Mystics in Washington. At that time, through the use of our *Healing Prayer* ritual, we invoke the spiritual forces from the higher spiritual realms and direct them to the students who have written in for various kinds of help, until their auras are filled to overflowing with the divine radiance of the spiritual power the service invokes. The names are also recorded by the Invisible Helpers, and special help of the kind best suited to the case is sent to each petitioning one often with marvelous results.

Prayer and Healing.—True prayer is an aspiration of the Soul for union with the Divine. All prayer to be effective must be accompanied by intense aspiration to contact God. It is a ray of spiritual force from the heart which penetrates up through all the lower realms of the invisible worlds to the spiritual realm with which it affinitizes, the highest the development of the aspirant can reach. But it has to reach up at least into the fourth sphere before it can contact the Higher Teachers, Masters, Devas and other angelic Beings. They will come down half way to meet you, but you must also reach up to meet them half way. This is why selfish and insincere prayers never reach higher-than the earthbound realms, hence are unanswered. For the angelic helpers have no knowledge of you and your needs until you tune in to the high vibrations of Their consciousness.

The Return Current.—Once make that contact and you bring down the return current from whatever realm you have contacted. As your aspiration passes upward through the various realms, its line of light attracts the attention, first of your loved ones who are interested in your welfare, then the higher angelic beings and those Great Ones who are assigned to that work, and finally reaches the consciousness of the Christ, focussed through the Master Jesus who is the head of the Healing Hierarchy. And He assigns to your help just those beings, persons and forces which can best meet your need, in accordance with karmic law. Throughout the history of mankind there has always been this tele-pathic communion with the Christ. His incarnations were only a part of His work.

Healing Prayer.—"Oh Thou loving and helpful Master Jesus! Thou who gavest to Thy disciples power to heal the sick! We, recognizing Thee, and realizing Thy divine presence with us, ask Thee to lay Thy hands upon us in healing love. Cleanse us from all our sins, and by the divine power of Omnipotent Life, drive out the atoms of inharmony and disease, and fill our bodies full to overflowing with Life, and Love and Purity."[3]

"If your eyes could be opened to see the effect the repetition of this prayer produces on the higher planes, the forces it brings to your aid, you would realize its beauty and its power. When you recite this prayer sincerely the angels crowd around you like flocks of doves, to ward off harmful forces and protect the germ of your physical, mental and spiritual life.

The One-Life.—"Upon the highest plane of Spirit, life is the One-Life which can be nothing but perfection. The repetition of this prayer is like a projectile fired through the earth's atmosphere creating a passage through which the One-Life must necessarily flow to you. As it passes from plane to plane it manifests upon the soul plane—the plane of

---

[3] *Prayers of the O. C. M.*, Curtiss, 8.

creation and of redemption—as spiritual love. When this spiritual love—the Son of God—reaches the physical plane, it manifests in the body as the Life-force. Thus the Christ manifests on the spiritual plane as the One-Life, on the soul plane as Love and on the physical plane as Life-force.

"This is the rationale of all healing, and a thorough recognition and realization of the presence of this life-force, and its working out in a three-fold manner, produces that harmony which is health to both mind and body. It also harmonizes conditions in your environment.

Condenses Aura.—"Negative emotions produce inharmony and sickness by condensing your aura and shutting out this force of life from you. If you send a thought of hatred toward a person you put a wall around yourself which only your own loving thoughts and prayers such as the above, can pierce and break down, and which shuts out the life-force from you and permits disease to flourish.

Jesus Answers.—"Jesus, the high Master who is at the head of the Healing Hierarchy, is ever ready to answer such a call as this prayer sends out. And it is only such a call that can pierce the clouds that hide the earthly from the Divine, and make a channel through which the divine healing forces can reach you.

"When you say 'lay Thy hands upon us in healing

love,' it is a literal adaptation of the words, 'Thou hast made Thine angels Thy handmaidens, and Thy ministers a flaming sword;' for the angelic hosts minister to all pure hearts who desire their help.

"The 'hands' which you ask the great Master to lay upon your head are His powers to accomplish, manifested through this host of angels who have the power to carry His divine force to you.

Help Desired.—"Whenever you desire help, physical, mental or spiritual, either for yourself or others, repeat this prayer, meditating on each word and trying to realize its true meaning on all planes of your being.

"As the Master Jesus gave to His disciples power to heal the sick, *and has never withdrawn that gift,* so every true disciple who firmly believes this, and faithfully strives to manifest the Christ Principle within him, has *now* the power, through the laying on of hands, (by the summoning of the angelic hosts), to bring this One-Life into manifestation, and thus relieve ills and promote health and harmony."[4]

Faith Healing.—"Faith is a Soul memory or inner conviction, even though inexplicable to the reasoning mind, that everything manifesting in the Cosmos comes from the Divine and descends through the various worlds and realms of expression

---

[4] *The Healing Prayer*, Chapter XXVI in *The Voice of Isis*, Curtiss.

to manifest ultimately here on earth according to exact law. The greater this realization, the greater the demonstration. 'According to thy faith be it onto thee.' Absolute faith in your oneness with the Divine enables the cosmic forces to flow into you and your affairs and solve all your problems for you, be it healing, guidance or supply. . . . Lack of faith makes the Soul anemic and lifeless. . . . Have faith that that which has been planted within shall grow and bring forth abundantly day by day, so that the substance of things hoped for shall become the manifested evidence of things not seen."[5]

Faith Needed.—Although Jesus said: "All things are possible to him that believeth,"[6] even He found faith in Him necessary on the part of the patient, for in His home town, "He did not many mighty works there *because of their unbelief.*"[7]

Quiet Time.—We have repeatedly urged you to make a period of prayer, of "morning quiet" and consecration, the most important engagement of the day. For it is an engagement to meet and correlate with the indwelling presence of the Christ, claiming His promise, "I am with you always," and relying on Him in absolute trust, *and in obedience* to His guidance, and believing in it (*Matt.* xxi, 22), (*St. John*, xiv, 13, 14), whether you consciously hear the

---

[5] Send for free copy of the lesson on *Faith*, Curtiss.
[6] *St. Mark*, ix, 23.
[7] *St. Matthew*, xiii, 58.

answer or not. If you do this, then you will be given the power. And it will be given in proportion to the intensity of your desire and your consecration to it. But to attain it you must be willing to let go of and *consciously give up* every known sin or inconsistency. You must maintain right relationships with all men; must willingly make amends for every unkind word and make restitution for every wrong done as soon as you are guided to do so. Only so can you be spiritually free, free from the overshadowing, hampering consciousness of inharmony not adjusted.

Discipline.—Keeping that morning tryst is a most practical exercise which pays big dividends in tangible, physical results, health and success. It is also *a test of the sincerity* of your desire for advancement. It is a test in self-discipline to see if you will get up ten minutes earlier and *take the extra time* for this communion and guidance. But to make it effective you must take the attitude of, "Speak Lord, for Thy servant heareth." Then you must wait, not tensely, but relaxed and quietly, as if listening to a loved voice, for the strongest impression or idea that comes.

How Test?—How can you tell that it is truly spiritual guidance? Test it by these standards. Does it go contrary to the highest standard or belief you already hold? Is it absolutely honest, pure,

unselfish and kind? Does it conflict with your recognized duties and responsibilities to others? If uncertain,
continue to pray silently during the day for light and
guidance on that problem, or you may talk it over with
some friend who also gets his guidance and can understand your need and give you corroboration. Also
write down the main ideas and impressions which arise
during your meditation. Then at night see how far they
have worked out.

In other words, look upon yourself not as a mere
mortal, but as a *spiritual being* who is making a short
tour of this world and who must render an account of
his activities in this outer world each night. By following this plan you will gain certain definite results in
the way, first, of positive guidance as to how to handle
the chief events of the day which you know confront
you, whether they be of a business or personal nature.
Also you will get reminders of things you should do;
errands, letters to write, visits to make, appointments
to keep, etc. You will get guidance concerning others
and your relation to them, sharing happy thoughts, saying kind, cheering words, doing unselfish deeds, etc.
You will also be given warnings what not to do, how
the Inner Radiance will protect you from undesirable
influences, etc.

Morning Prayer.—Remember the *Morning
Prayer*: "I have within me the power of the Christ.

I can conquer all that comes to me today. I am strong enough to bear every trial and *accept every joy* and to say 'Thy will be done.' Amen."[8]

A Changed Life.—If health and long life are thus restored to you, what will you do with them? Will you go on living the same old thoughtless, selfish, aimless, unplanned life? Will you go on making the same old mistakes and suffering from the same old results? Or will you profit by the help offered you by this book and henceforth live a changed life, not only physically, but mentally, morally, socially and spiritually?

Know and Do.—It is not enough for you merely to know the principles and laws of life presented herein. If they are of any importance to you, then you will *put them into practice.* That means a changed mode of life for you, changed habits, changed mode of thought, motives, actions.

Decide Now.—Make up your mind definitely to follow religiously the suggestions given herein. For no matter how good they are, they will do you no good unless you apply them. Therefore, make them a definite part of your daily routine, more important than your meals. And the rewards which Nature and the Great Law will give you will be beyond price.

Your Reactions.—Why wait until you pass on

---

[8] *Prayers of the O. C. M.*, Curtiss, 3.

from this life to look over, recognize and correct your mistakes? Why not do it now and save the unnecessary suffering you will otherwise have to pass through? Never mind how others react to a knowledge of the Law. *Your reaction* is the important thing. Therefore, determine that *you* will live up to the knowledge you have gained and henceforth will work with the Law, or let the Law work through and for you.

An Important Decision.—Today for you is the most important day of your life, thus far. You have been entrusted with all the information contained herein, and you will be held responsible for the use or lack of use you make of it. Therefore, *decide today*. By deciding favorably you can look forward to a prolonged, useful and happy life, free from bodily ills and mental worries and other handicaps to the manifestation of your *Real Self* and living your real life.

Origin Divine.—As we have said elsewhere: "Our body is, indeed, an advanced animal organism, the most advanced of the whole animal kingdom. But it is far more than an advanced animal, for it has been evolved[9] and prepared for a special purpose, namely, the manifestation in the physical world of a divine and spiritual Being who is far above the animal kingdom, the Spiritual Man made

---

[9] See *Evolution and the Bible*, Curtiss, Chapters iii, v, xix.

in the image of God and eternal in the heavens, and whose home or center of force—like all centers of force—is in the invisible realms, in this case in the Spiritual World as explained above. It is through this intimate relationship between the Spiritual Self and its animal instrument of expression that the animal becomes the earthly dwelling place of that Divine Self. And within this instrument the Christ-consciousness must dwell, even though at first it must rest almost dormant, like a babe wrapped in swaddling clothes, waiting until the spiritual radio-activity of His presence can gradually uplift our consciousness and our thoughts and aspirations into a great longing for Divinity, and finally into a great realization of His actual presence within us. . . . And through these powers that Higher Self must learn to control the animal organism and lift it up until it is an efficient and obedient servant of the Christ within. Then it will in truth be a temple of the living God. This is the great lesson for us to learn.

Real Self.—"We will then realize that the Real Self is never inharmonious, angry, ill or discouraged. All those emotions and inharmonious conditions arise within the body or the consciousness of the personal self. And when they arise, if we turn to the Christ within at once, He will give us the power to conquer and redeem them. We must, of course, utilize the functions and powers of the animal body, but *must control them* and not allow them to dominate us. We must eat and drink, not because we love to eat and drink—although we should enjoy doing so—but that our physical body may be a healthy, happy animal, a more nearly perfect instrument for our use. We must protect it not only from physical harm, but also from the devastating storms of inharmony, antagonism, anger and other destructive emotions, and also from the poisonous effects of incorrect eating and of impure thoughts, so that our body shall be kept as a holy temple, so pure, clean, harmonious and holy that the Divine Self will have little difficulty in manifestating through it. . . . Then His radiance will flow outward and pervade our whole nature, purifying, uplifting and blessing it and making our whole body in very truth *a temple of the Living God* wherein dwelleth righteousness."[10]

May the following of the teachings given herein be a source of purification, understanding, health, harmony, happiness and blessing to you.

---

[10] Send for free copy of the lesson *The Holy Temple*, Curtiss.

Food Combinations.—Any food in column 1 or in column 3 may be combined with any food in column 2. But do *NOT* combine any food in column 1 with any food in column 3, with the exceptions that honey, being a natural sweet, may be combined with fruits, and that almonds may be combined with any other food, as they are alkaline-forming.

1	2	3
CARBOHYDRATES STARCHES	FATS	PROTEINS
Artichokes	Animal	Cheese
Bananas	Avocadoes	Eggs
Beans, (dried)	Bacon	Game
Breads	Butter	Gelatin
Cereals	Cocoanut	Meats
Corn	Cod liver oil	Milk
Flour Products	Cream	Nuts (except
Pastries	Egg Yolks	chestnuts and
Peanuts	Lard	peanuts)
Peas, (dried)	Oily Nuts	All Sea Food
Popcorn	Vegetable Oils	
Potatoes		
Pumpkin		
Rice (polished)		
Sago		
Squash (winter)		
Tapioca		
Only one item at a meal		

ALKALINE-BASE FOODS

VEGETABLES

SWEETS	*Roots*	*Green (con't)*	FRUITS*
Candy	Beets	Corn on Cob	Apples
Dates	Carrots	Cress	Apricots
Figs	Celery Root	Cucumbers	Avocado
Honey	Kohlrabi	Dandelion	Berries (all
Ice Cream	Mangel-wurtzel	Dulce	except
Maple Sugar	Mushrooms	Egg plant	Cranberries)
Molasses	Onions	Endive	Bananas (dark
Preserves	Parsnips	Green Peppers	skin)
Raisins	Radishes	Green Peas	Cherries
Sugar	Salsify	Kale	Currants
Syrups	Turnips	Lettuce	Dates
		Okra	Figs
Take milk with fruits and vegetables only.	*Green*	Olives	Grapes
	Asparagus	Parsely	Grapefruit
	Beans (string)	Pimento	Lemons
	Beet tops	Pumpkin	Melons
Choose over 3/4 (80%) of your food from among the vegetables and fruits.	Brussels sprouts	Rhubarb	Oranges
	Brocolli	Spinach	Peaches
	Cabbage	Swisschard	Pears
	Cauliflower	Squash	Persimmons
	Celery	Sauerkraut	Pineapple
	Chicory	Tomatoes (uncooked)	Prune (small)
		Turnips	Raisins
			Tangerines

* Fresh or dried - all kinds (except Plums)

SUGGESTIVE MENUS
of compatible combinations

BREAKFAST SUGGESTIONS

Sedentary Persons
Fresh fruit or fruit juices (unsweetened) or occasional toast and coffee with cream and sugar, if greatly desired or if weather is very cold.

Active Persons
Crisp fat bacon, three or four slices of toasted or stale whole wheat, rye or graham bread, well buttered and with honey if desired. Or

Whole grain pancakes or waffles with maple syrup or honey and coffee, cream and sugar.

Soaked figs or dates may be added to either of the above breakfasts.

LUNCHEON

Monday
Cream of mushroom soup
Fresh beans steamed
Salad: Roman lettuce with French dressing[1]
Dessert: Orange and grapefruit sections with whipped cream.

DINNER

Monday
Vegetable broth
Roast chicken or broilers
Steamed carrots
Steamed spinach
Salad: Tomato, cucumber, watercress with ripe olives and mayonnaise[2]
Dessert: Fresh red grapes.

---

[1] Always use lemon juice instead of vinegar.
[2] May be flavored with pineapple juice, but when used with a starch meal sauerkraut juice may be used in place of lemon or pineapple juice.

Hard workers may add: Baked Potato, Crisp Fat Bacon.

Tuesday	*Tuesday*
Cream of onion Soup [1]	Tomato juice
Steamed spinach (chopped fine)	Roast beef
	Brussels sprouts steamed
Salad: Cooked string beans, green peppers and tomato, with French dressing	Steamed wax beans
	Salad: Shredded cabbage, apple, chopped mushrooms and celery or raw spinach leaves with mayonnaise.
Dessert: Baked apples with cream.	*Dessert*: Fresh pears.

Hard workers may add: Baked potato, sliced onions.

Dessert: Date ice cream.

Wednesday	*Wednesday*
Tomato soup	Cream of mushroom soup
Steamed celery root	Hashed brown potato with onion
Salad: Shredded carrot and parsnips with mayonnaise.	Crisp fat bacon
	Steamed celery
Dessert: Fresh green grapes.	*Salad:* Tomato with whipped cream
	Dessert: Maple ice cream.

Hard workers may add: Broiled T bone steak at lunch.

Thursday	*Thursday*
Cream of beet soup	Vegetable soup
Steamed celery and leek	Roast Lamb. Baked onion

---

[1] Various cream soups may be made with 1/3 cup of the vegetable chosen, 1/3 cup of water and 1/3 cup of cream. Season with vegetable salt.

Salad: Combination vegetable
Dessert: Shredded pears in whipped cream with nuts.

Baked egg plant
Salad: Beet, bean, carrot, pea and celery with French dressing.
Desert: Apple Sauce with whipped cream sweetened with honey or raisins.

Hard workers may add: Whole wheat macaroni, Lettuce and onion salad with oil, dates and cream.

Friday
Cream of pea soup
Broccoli with Hollandaise sauce
Salad: Green pepper, tomato and bermuda onion with French dressing
Dessert: Slices Pineapple.

Friday
Vegetable broth
Broiled halibut or steak
Steamed endive
Buttered carrots
Salad: Cabbage, apple, celery and raisin with mayonnaise
Dessert: Peaches and cream.

Hard workers may add : Buttered whole wheat toast, Sour cream cookies.

Saturday
Cream of spinach soup
Steamed wax beans with mushrooms
Salad: Lettuce with pimento dressing
Dessert: Raw apple.

Saturday
Cream of pea soup
Mashed Potato
Sauerkraut
Bacon (if desired)
Celery & radishes
Dessert: Baked custard with maple syrup.

With lunch hard workers may add: hot sliced meat.

Sunday
Cream of parsnip soup
Fresh asparagus on toast
Salad: Tomato with
  whipped cream
Dessert: Frozen custard.

Sunday
Tomato juice
Broiled live lobster
Steamed fresh green
  beans
Steamed broccoli
Salad: Lettuce with
  French dressing
Dessert: Fresh fruit cup
  Demitasse.

Hard workers may add: Cookies.

~

Menus from the Sun-Diet Health Service[1]

Breakfast is preferably composed of fruit and milk or else some form of whole grain breadstuff with sweet fruit, or figs, dates or raisins.

LUNCH

DINNER

Monday
Scalloped potatoes with
  onion
Mashed turnips
Asparagus tips on lettuce
  with oil dressing
Dates.

Monday
Vegetable soup
Poached eggs
Brussels sprouts
Rutabagas
Salad of lettuce, apples,
  and raisins with
  whipped cream
California grapes.

Tuesday
Toasted whole wheat
  bread with butter

Tuesday
Carrot and onion soup
Lamb chops

---

[1] *The Master Key to Health*, Alsaker.

Steamed carrots
Baked eggplant
Cabbage and celery
  salad dressed with oil
Raisins and almonds.

Cauliflower with butter
  sauce
Peas
Salad of lettuce, orange
  and pineapple with
  lemon mayonnaise
Apricot whip, with
  honey.

Wednesday
Cooked brown rice with
  cream
Buttered beets
Spinach
Salad of asparagus
  tips on lettuce with
  whipped cream
Sweet pears.

Wednesday
Vegetable broth
Egg omelet
Baked onions
Steamed green cabbage
Salad of lettuce and
  French endive with
  lemon mayonnaise
Baked apple or figs.

Thursday
Baked potato
Steamed turnips
Carrots
Salad of lettuce, cucum-
  bers and radishes, oil
  dressing
Date ice cream.

Thursday
Cream of celery soup
Cauliflower
String beans
Salad of raisins and
  grated carrots with
  dressing of lemon
  juice and oil
Sweet pears.

Friday
Broiled mushrooms on
  whole wheat toast
Steamed broccoli
Green peas

Friday
Vegetable soup
Broiled fish
Tomatoes and okra
Spinach

Salad of lettuce, shredded cabbage and
celery with lemon and
oil dressing
Sliced bananas

Saturday
Whole wheat raisin toast
Cauliflower
Buttered beets
Salad of grated carrots
on lettuce leaves with
oil
Malaga Grapes.

SUNDAY

Dinner
Relish of ripe olives and
celery hearts
Vegetable soup
Roast chicken
Spinach
String beans
Salad of sliced tomatoes
on lettuce leaves with
lemon mayonnaise
Peach ice cream.

Salad of orange and
grapefruit on let-
tuce with lemon
mayonnaise
Baked apple with cream.

Saturday
Cream of asparagus
soup
Parsley omelet
Rutabagas
Steamed onions
Salad of lettuce with pi-
mento dressing
Stewed figs.

SUNDAY

Supper
Whole wheat muffins
Steamed carrots and
peas
Salad of lettuce and
asparagus tips with
dressing of whipped
cream and oil
Raisins.

SHORT BIBLIOGRAPHY

WORKS OF DR. WILLIAM HOWARD HAY:
Hay System News, Monthly
Kitchen Food Chart
Medical Millennium
New Health Era
Official Cook Book
Pocket Guide

OTHER IMPORTANT WORKS:
Acid-Base Balance of the Body, BiSoDol Co.
Advantages of Raw Food, Dr. Julian P. Thomas.
Dr. Beal, or More About the Unseen, E. M. S.
Grape Cure, Mrs. Johanna Brandt.
Fasting Book, Mrs. Johanna Brandt.
Fasting and Man's Correct Diet, R. B. Pearson.
Fasting for the Cure of Disease, Dr. Linda B. Hazzard.
Fasting, Hydropathy and Exercise, Dr. F. Oswald.
Hindu Dietetics, Sri Deva Ram Sukul.
House of Wonder, E. M. S.
How to Live, Prof. Irving Fisher & Dr. E. L. Fisk.

Master Key to Health, Dr. Rasmus Alsaker.
Nature Cure, Dr. H. Lindhlahr.
One Thing I Know, E. M. S.
Ortho Dietetics, Henry James Broughton.
Perfect Sight Without Glasses, Dr. W. H. Bates.
Royal Road to Health, Dr. Chas. A. Tyrrell.
Sun Diet Cook Book, Anna Lana Alsaker.
True Science of Living, Dr. E. H. Dewey.
Universal Health Restorer, Veni Cooper-Mathieson.
Vitality, Fasting and Nutrition, H. C. Carrington.

INDEX

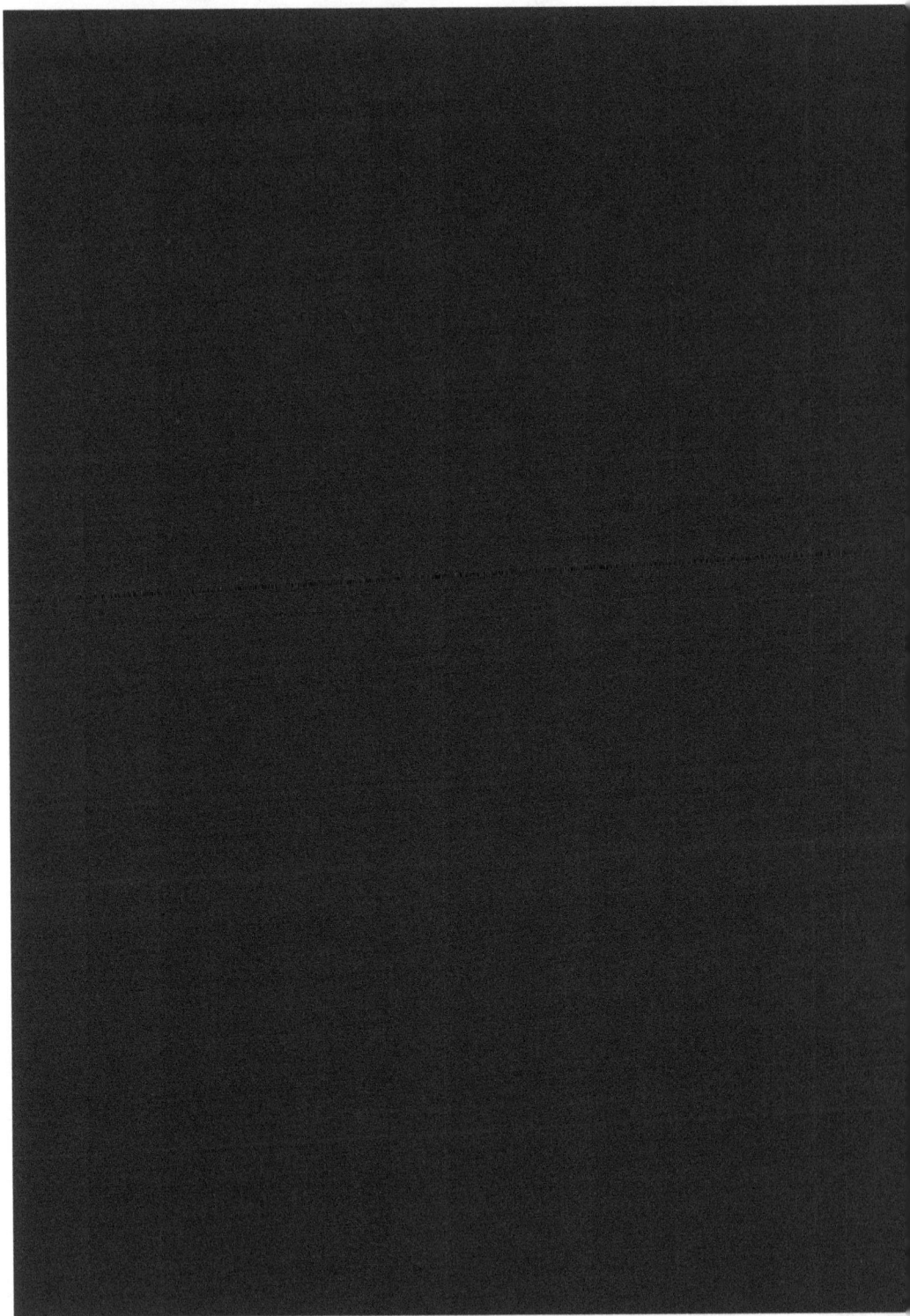

www.ingramcontent.com/pod-product-compliance
Lightning Source LLC
Chambersburg PA
CBHW061736020426
42331CB00006B/1264